International Trade and Globalisation

Fourth Edition

Dr. Charles Smith

Swansea School of Education
Swansea Metropolitan University

Dedication

For my beautiful grand-daughters Seren and Abi.

Also for their extended family in places all around
this little globe of just 8000 miles of rock.

© Anforme Ltd 2010
ISBN 978-1-905504-38-1
Anforme Ltd, Stocksfield Hall, Stocksfield, Northumberland NE43 7TN.
Typeset by George Wishart & Associates, Whitley Bay.
Printed by Potts, Cramlington.

Contents

Preface and acknowledgements

The first edition of this book was entitled *Understanding International Trade*. In order to reflect current debate, and in order to cater for the demands of re-structured examination syllabuses, the idea of the 'global' was incorporated into the title of the second edition: *International Trade and Globalisation* and further consideration was given to the role of globalisation in modern economic activity.

The basic structure of the book has proved tremendously popular with teachers and students, and so in subsequent editions this has been largely unchanged, apart from essential updating, while additional sections and chapters have been added to take account of new developments, and to put further stress on the phenomenon of globalisation. With respect to trade, if not with respect to power politics and militarism, this phenomenon– now appears to be rather less synonymous with 'Americanisation', and must now take account of the remarkable developments taking place elsewhere, in countries like China and India. While the world moves on rapidly, it also moves in great circles. Often we fail to learn from history. For example, when planning this Fourth Edition, it was intended to remove the section in Chapter 11 on the economic collapse of the so-called 'Tiger' economies in 1997. However, the Credit Crunch of 2008 and the ensuing recession, according to some politicians and economists came from nowhere, was unprecedented, and totally unexpected. It affected large economies like the USA, medium sized economies like the UK, small countries like Iceland, and even rocked the 'Celtic Tiger' of Ireland. So it was decided that this section still had some relevance after all, as a reminder that history has not ended, and one of the worst things we can do is make grand announcements, for example that we have abolished 'boom and bust', when in fact we have not remembered essential lessons from the past.

A brief stroll round the average supermarket is enough to convince even the most casual observer that society is becoming more and more internationalised. Products that just ten or fifteen years ago were unheard of in this country are now commonplace. Items that once were expensive luxuries are now regarded as basic necessities. My mother, who came to Britain from Spain in 1947, remembered a time when olive oil was available over here only from the chemist's shop, for medicinal purposes. Once, after a visit to Spain in the 1970s, my wife and I tried to find some squid in our town's provisions market. The fishmonger looked at us as if we were Martians and pointed to a bucket containing this item which, he reckoned, was only in demand by local sea anglers who used it as bait.

There must be thousands of examples of how the rare, the exotic and the 'foreign' have become routine, familiar and domesticated. Even the seasons appear to have been eliminated, with transport and delivery systems enabling perishables to become available all the year round.

Every November the world's largest container ships edge into Felixstowe harbour, full of goods from China, ready to flood the shelves of retailers for the UK Christmas market. We are told that our future lies in services: but look at the goods on sale in the High Street or out-of-town retail sheds: clothes, electrical items, gadgets and gizmos. All this stuff comes in containers from all around the world. It appears that our appetite for such goods is insatiable, and yet we are deliberately giving up our ability to manufacture them. What is going on?

The word 'globalisation' has come to be repeated like a mantra, and we are told by people who rarely attempt to explain its meaning (probably because they do not understand it themselves) that we must accept its implications without question. The time is ripe for a re-evaluation of this concept, and this book attempts to argue that far from being a basic fact of life, or an iron law of nature, globalisation is a contestable concept, whose time has come to be contested.

The very nature of our chosen subject, economics, is both international and global, and yet many textbooks discuss international trade and globalisation as afterthoughts, and some even ignore these issue areas altogether.

Quite rightly, international trade is a core topic area in ' A' Level Economics. It is an essential part of the International Baccalaureate programme, and also figures largely in Business Studies syllabuses and in higher education Economics, Business degree programmes and MBAs. Recent and forthcoming syllabus developments confirm this central position. This booklet aims to assist teachers and lecturers to reinforce the teaching and learning of this topic area by covering the main issues in a way which is up-to-date and relevant. It is hoped that it will help the reader to improve understanding of the main complexities, make linkages between international trade, globalisation and other parts of the framework of economics, approach core examination topics with confidence, and follow current debate with a critical awareness.

Although the main purpose of this book is to examine international trade and globalisation from the UK perspective, a wholly anglo-centric point of view would be totally inconsistent with the 'internationalism' which modern economists must imbibe and adopt as second nature. Some of the chapters therefore attempt to inject a little empathy for wider perspectives.

Economics is at once exasperating and fascinating due to its constant change and evolution. For this book, my main sources of recent statistics for the international trading position of the UK have been the printed publications of the Office of National Statistics. In the UK the 'open government' website is becoming increasingly useful as a source of up-to-date information. Eurostat is the main source of EU statistics. The World Bank's *World Development Report* and the United Nations Development Programme's *Human Development Report* (both annual publications) are also essential sources for students and teachers. Websites such as nationmaster.com have become invaluable for international comparisons. Every effort has been made to acknowledge sources, but if any have been overlooked or wrongly attributed this will be rectified at the earliest opportunity.

What makes the teaching of economics so frustrating for some, and such a challenge for others, is that educationists in this field have to be always learning, thinking, and modifying their ideas, and I have derived great benefit from debates and discussions with colleagues and friends at home and abroad which have helped select themes for this book. I particularly wish to thank Gareth Rees, United World College of the Atlantic, and Peter Nicols, University of New South Wales, for previous collaborations which have helped to inform and underpin important parts of my current work. I have learned a lot about relationships between the global and local from Professor Sean Loughlin of Cardiff University and Dr. Jörg Mathias of the University of Aston, and their expert influence has helped greatly in my own struggle to understand some important processes and paradigms.

An advantage of the 'booklet' format in which this work appears is that it is possible to up-date regularly, keeping the format and structure as constant as possible for the benefit of long-term users, but revising sections of the content in line with contemporary facts and issues. This is especially desirable in the field of international trade and globalisation where traditional heavy textbooks are habitually out-dated before their ink is even dry. For the benefit of future editions the author would be very pleased to receive constructive criticism and suggestions from users, whether they be teachers, lecturers, examiners or students on any items of controversy, not least some of the predictions contained in the final chapter. Having mentioned revised editions I wish to thank Nigel Tree and his team at Anforme for their continued commitment to this publication. Special thanks are due to Peter Maunder, now retired from Loughborough University, for his perceptive editing.

None of the above mentioned persons or institutions should be associated with any errors or omissions. These are all my own responsibility.

C.E.S.

Chapter 1
What is international trade?

UK plc

Globalisation is closely associated with what is known as 'free trade'. It is often said that the UK is a 'trading nation'. It is regarded as a fact of life that **open economies** (those which trade freely with the outside world) are more successful than **closed economies** (those which protect themselves against international competition). Politicians have been heard to say that countries must 'export or die'. All the world's major economies belong to an organisation called the 'World Trade Organisation', which exists in order to foster international trade. What is **international trade** and why is it important?

International trade involves the **exchange** of goods and services between one country and another. Sometimes there is a direct exchange of goods for goods, a system known as **barter**, but in modern economies the 'exchange' usually takes place indirectly, with items being sold for a money payment and the money then being exchanged for items which are bought. Where countries have different currencies, it is therefore important for these currencies themselves to be tradable (or 'convertible'), and to have a price against other currencies. This 'price' is known as an **exchange rate**, and has an important influence on international trade.

Although we talk of 'international' trade, it is important to realise that trade does not really take place between 'nations' as such. It actually takes place between **economic agents** or decision makers within nations, such as individuals, families, or businesses. Some items (certain pieces of defence equipment, for example) might be traded between governments acting as economic agents and the government might take a high profile in encouraging and regulating trade. But on the whole most international trade takes place not between governments but private-sector decision makers who just happen to be located within different nations. So, for example, when a British family decides to buy a Japanese car, or insures the car with a French insurance company, or takes the car on a holiday in Spain, these decisions result in international trade. We might not tend to think of a foreign holiday as resulting in international trade, but what happens when a British family goes to Spain is that they purchase travel and hotel services from Spanish companies. In effect, a tourism service has been exported from Spain and imported to the UK.

Where trade is in a physical item (such as raw materials or manufactured products) it is classed as **visible** trade; where there is trade in services (such as banking, tourism and insurance) we refer to **invisible** trade.

Table 1.1: Contribution to UK GDP of industrial sectors (2008)

Agriculture	1%
Manufacturing	23%
Services	76%

Source: ONS

The UK used to be famous for its visible exports, particularly its manufactured products. The UK was the first country to go through an industrial revolution, and in the nineteenth century became known as the 'workshop of the world'. Today, the relative size of the UK's manufacturing export sector has declined as Table 1.1 makes clear.

After the Second World War the UK experienced economic growth and a general rise in living standards which were both more rapid than anything experienced by previous generations. At the same time, however, there was a *relative* decline in economic performance when compared with other western countries, and some countries around the Pacific rim also.

In 1850 the British economy was the largest in the world, measured by GDP, and Britain produced 41% of the world's manufactured exports. By the year 2000 this had fallen to 5%. However, manufacturers

continue to make a sizeable contribution to an economy that is heavily involved in international trade, providing 60% of the UK's exports. But the economic influence of the manufacturing sector is slowly dwindling. Just after World War II, for example, manufacturing accounted for almost 40% of the UK economy. The sector also employs considerably less people than it used it. At the end of the 1970s, it employed just under a third of the total UK workforce. And in 2009 alone, an estimated 150,000 manufacturing jobs were lost.

As it gradually came on stream during the 1970s, many saw North Sea oil as a major national resource, and hoped that exports of this commodity would restore the UK's international position. Yet by the early 1990s the UK balance of payments had begun to show record deficits – and North Sea oil was actually partly to blame. Oil exports increased the value of the pound against other currencies, which in turn put manufacturing exporters under pressure by increasing their export prices.

With the exhaustion of the North Sea oil field, In the late 1990s and 2000s the financial industry was seen by some as a future motor of economic growth and employment in the UK. Ironically, monetary policy replaced oil exports as a handicap on British manufacturing exporters. Many experts repeatedly claimed that interest rates could have been lowered without necessarily causing inflation, and that as a result the pound was over-valued against other currencies.

Because of the strength of its service sector, and particularly because of the large annual flow of financial assets through the City of London, the UK registers as the fourth to sixth largest economy in the world (depending on the measurement methods used), and this type of statistic is often quoted by politicians.

Table 1.2: UK's national income world rankings

	GDP	GDP per head
1946	3	3
1966	3	18
1986	6	25
2006	6	13

Sources: OECD; *British Historical Statistics*, Macmillan; *Human Development Report 2003*, www.undp.org; nationmaster.com

However, in terms of Gross Domestic Product (national income) per head, which is usually regarded as an important indicator of living standards, the UK is lower down the world league tables. It should also be noted that GDP per head is a raw average, and that most economic measures indicate that income distribution within the UK has become less equal over the last decade.

Some commentators have claimed that the UK must become an enterprise economy. Certain politicians are very obviously a great admirer of the 'enterprising' attitudes claimed by the private sector. An essential requirement of any enterprise is that it should be able to 'balance' its books. In later chapters we consider the extent to which 'UK plc' can be considered a successful enterprise if it cannot balance its international payments. Does this balancing act really matter? We consider this question in Chapter 3.

What goods and services does the UK trade in?

A familiar pattern has long been recognised by economists: as an economy develops its primary sector (agriculture, extraction) tends to get smaller as a proportion of total national output and employment, while the secondary sector (manufacture, construction) gets larger. Then gradually the tertiary sector (services) becomes the largest of all. This pattern can be recognised in the UK's international trade profile, and is also reflected in the fact that Britain has a trade gap (it spends more on imports than it earns from exports).

Some people believe that the UK is now a 'service centre' rather than a 'workshop', and while it is certainly true that a deficit in visible trade has often been compensated for by a surplus on invisibles, it can be argued that the UK's manufacturing decline has been accompanied by a fall in its position in world economic league tables in general, suggesting that modern economies need to achieve good performance in a *balance* of sectors in order to achieve high living standards. There is certainly a high demand for services in the UK, but there is also a high demand for goods. To many, it seems defeatist to accept that

Table 1.3: UK trade in goods and services, credits less debits (£m)

Year	Goods	Services	Total goods and services	Current balance (includes investment income and other current transfers)	Current balance as % of GDP
1954	-210	115	-95	160	0.9
1979	-3326	4573	1247	-1002	-0.5
2008	-92876	48878	-43998	-24493	-1.7

Source: ONS, *Annual Abstract of Statistics*, 2009

those goods should all be imported, and it appears to suggest that the destiny for many of our workers is to be consigned to relatively low-wage jobs in the retail trade, where customers purchase products where most of the real value was added in other parts of the world.

Is manufacturing unimportant, and does our future lie in services? Perhaps what is really important is the **'value-added'** in an economy. It is possible to have low-grade manufacturing, where workers merely assemble components designed elsewhere for products invented and ultimately marketed elsewhere. It is far better to be involved in the high 'value-added' activities of invention, design and marketing. Similarly, many jobs in the service sector are of low quality, involving unskilled part-time work, often on short-term contracts at or near the minimum wage. 'Services' cover a multitude of sins, and if our future is in this sector, then we should aim to be involved in high value-added activities. Designing computer systems involves more value-added than selling computers from a high street store.

During the 1990s a worrying trend emerged, whereby manufacturers in the UK closed their British manufacturing facilities and transferred them to low-wage countries. Loss-making toy manufacturers, such as the world famous Hornby Trains, became profitable once more by making their mass-produced models in China instead of in Margate, Kent. The Dyson Company, famous for its 'bagless' vacuum cleaners and synonymous with British entrepreneurship, inventive flair and imaginative design, gravely disappointed many of its admirers by 'exporting jobs' to Asia from its base in Malmesbury, Wiltshire.

What is really important is the 'value added' in an economy.

The response of many politicians was to say, in effect: 'Never mind, our workers are flexible and can re-train for jobs in service industries such as computing and ICT (information and communication technology).' This position has become seriously undermined in the early years of the 21st Century by another worrying trend: large institutions such as British Telecom, HSBC and Lloyds TSB have been moving call centres and computer services to countries such as India, where English language and ICT skills are well developed, but far less well financially rewarded than in the UK.

Who does the UK trade with?

It is sometimes claimed that the UK has 'more in common' with the economies of the USA and Canada than with those of Europe. However, it can be argued that is an impression rather than a reality. The impression is created by the influence of the 'monetary' economy rather than the 'real' economy. As an important financial centre, London is an important staging post for monetary movements, most of which are in dollars. This means that UK stock and monetary markets are very much 'in phase' with north American business cycles. However, while the world of monetary movements is important, it is not as vital to the everyday lives of average citizens as the **real economy** of employment, output, and spending. We therefore should *not* conclude that the UK's future lies in some sort of north Atlantic trading association rather than in the European Union (EU). Although this is an idea that has been promoted by some sections of the UK press, most economists would regard the idea as unrealistic. In terms of the real economy the trend is clearly towards ever closer links with the EU.

Table 1.4: Main trading partners of the UK, 2007

	% volume of exports		% volume of imports
USA	15	Germany	14
Germany	11	USA	9
France	10	China	7
Ireland	7	Netherlands	7
Netherlands	6	France	7
Belgium	6	Belgium	5
Spain	5	Norway	5
Italy	4	Italy	4

Source: ONS

Taking the value of imports and exports together, Table 1.4 shows that well over 50% of UK trade is now with other members of the EU, with the rest of its trade divided more or less equally between the rest of Europe, the North Atlantic Free Trade Area, and the rest of the world. The proportion of trade with the rest of the EU is gradually increasing. At the same time, industrial structures between the UK and the continent are becoming increasingly integrated; for example mergers between British and German car manufacturers, British retail stores trading in continental city centres, and Spanish companies taking control of British companies including banks and airports.

Chapter 2

Why does trade take place?

The importance of trade

International trade takes place *between* countries. Domestic trade takes place *within* countries. Is there really much of a difference? Should trade between the UK and other members of the EU be regarded as international or domestic?

As mentioned in Chapter 1, in an important sense there is no such thing as trade between nations. What actually happens is that *persons* make decisions that result in trade. These persons, sometimes known as *economic agents*, might be individuals, or they might represent organisations or institutions, such as businesses or departments of local or state governments. Thus when we say that international trade takes place, what we really mean is that goods and services are being exchanged between economic agents who happen to be located in different nation states.

All trade, whether domestic or national, takes place because of **specialisation**. Individual people specialise. Companies specialise. Historically, towns, cities and regions have specialised, at least to some extent. And countries also tend to specialise. Back in 1776 the Scottish economist Adam Smith referred to this as the **division of labour** and demonstrated that specialisation leads to increased efficiency, higher incomes and improved living standards. When people specialise, they become more and more skilled in a narrow range of tasks. This increases efficiency and output. It reduces prices and so increases real incomes.

Economists argue that trade takes place because of *comparative advantage*, a phrase coined by David Ricardo, a British economist of the early 19th Century. The law of comparative advantage states that:

> *'Countries will specialise in the production of those items in which their comparative advantage is greatest.'*

In order to understand this law, we must distinguish between absolute advantage and comparative advantage.

A country has an **absolute advantage** over another in the production of an item if, with a given amount of resources, it can produce more of that item than the other country. In other words, it can produce a unit of the item at a lower **factor cost** (cost measured in terms of productive resources used up). A country has a **comparative advantage** over another in the production of an item if it can produce that item at a lower **opportunity cost** (cost measured in terms of alternative items which could have been produced with the same productive resources).

The difference between absolute and comparative advantage is not obvious, and so Ricardo's insight is a very important and subtle one. In the days of Ricardo trading ships raced across the seas, and the purpose of trade was very clear. They sailed to, say, the far east with something the British had and the people of the far east wanted, such as wool or machine tools, and returned with something made in the far east which the British wanted, such as tea or silk. The whole point of trade was to allow an economy to *specialise*. Merchants in those days knew something which modern trade negotiators these days often seem to have forgotten. When Americans argue that Europe should buy American beef (even if it is hormone treated), because Americans buy European beef, then they are, in effect, arguing that beef should be traded for beef. Merchants of the nineteenth century would not have been very excited about trading silk for silk or rice for rice.

Ricardo's insight suggests to us that if a country is better at making cars than bikes, then it should put more resources into cars, and export some of the cars in exchange for bikes. This is even true if the country

happens to make the world's best bikes, for it will still benefit by making cars instead. Countries can therefore trade successfully, and prosper, without actually being the world's best at anything. Thus the world's best car might arguably be a British Rolls Royce, or an Italian Ferrari. But the Japanese prosper in car production because their production techniques have improved their efficiency so much that they are better at producing cars than other things, and Japan uses its car export revenues to buy things it is less good at making, such as Jumbo Jets. Companies exporting cars to Japan find it hard to compete unless they can send them a different sort of car: an Aston Martin, for example, as opposed to a mass produced middle-sized car.

Economists often use a simple numerical example to show the law of comparative advantage at work. One such example is shown in Figure 2.1.

Figure 2.1: How specialisation can make trade worthwhile

Table 1: Output before specialisation

	Apples		Bananas
Fredonia	10	+	5
Wilmania	9	+	3
Total world output	19	+	8

Table 4: Output after specialisation

	Apples		Bananas
Fredonia	–		10
Wilmania	18		–
Total world output	18	+	10

Table 2: Opportunity cost ratios for bananas

	Apples		Bananas
Fredonia	2	:	1
Wilmania	3	:	1

Table 5: After international trade

	Apples		Bananas
Fredonia	7.5	+	7
Wilmania	10.5	+	3
Total world output	18	+	10

Table 3: Opportunity cost ratios for apples

	Apples		Bananas
Fredonia	1	:	0.5
Wilmania	1	:	0.3

Let us assume that the world consists of two countries, Fredonia and Wilmania, and that these two countries can each produce two products: apples and bananas. Suppose each country starts with two *units of productive resource* each. A unit of productive resource (or 'UPR') represents a certain quantity of factors of production, or in other words, a given amount of land, labour, capital and enterprise that can be combined to produce an output. To begin with, suppose that each country devotes 1 UPR to each product. Within Figure 2.1, Table 1 shows the quantities of apples and bananas produced.

Let us say that to begin with, Fredonia produces 10 apples plus 5 bananas, while Wilmania produces 9 apples and 3 bananas. Total world output is therefore 19 apples plus 8 bananas.

Notice that with 1 UPR, Fredonia is able to produce more apples and more bananas than Wilmania. This means that Fredonia has an **absolute advantage** in both products. What does this mean to Wilmania? Does it mean that Wilmania is so inefficient that it cannot compete with Fredonia, and should just give up, perhaps becoming a colony of the more powerful country? The answer is 'no', because what is really important in this situation is not absolute but **comparative advantage**.

Now consider Table 2. Here we are looking at the ratio of apples to bananas for each country, and have reduced the banana output to 1 in order to make a comparison of the opportunity cost of producing a banana in each country. We see that each time Fredonia produces a banana, the world loses 2 apples.

However, when Wilmania produces a banana, the world loses 3 apples. Comparative advantage exists where the opportunity cost is lowest, and so we see that Fredonia has the comparative advantage in producing bananas. We can therefore assume that Wilmania has the comparative advantage in producing apples and we can demonstrate this numerically as in Table 3.

Here we have taken the data in Table 1, and reduced the figures for apples to 1, in order to compare opportunity costs of producing an apple in each country. We see that every time Fredonia produces an apple, the world loses half a banana (0.5), and every time Wilmania produces an apple, the world loses a third of a banana (approximately 0.3). The opportunity cost is therefore lower if Wilmania produces apples, therefore Wilmania has the comparative advantage in producing apples.

Suppose now that each country specialises in the product in which it has a comparative advantage. Each country can therefore produce twice as much of its specialised product, because it can devote 2 UPRs to this product instead of 1 UPR. The results are shown in Table 4.

Comparing Table 4 with Table 1 we can see the **gains from specialisation**. The world is better off by 2 bananas, but worse off by 1 apple. We will consider below whether this means that the world is on balance better off.

Since Fredonia now has no apples and Wilmania has no bananas, the two countries now need to trade. We need to consider the **terms of trade**, or the price of apples in terms of bananas. If we examine the opportunity cost ratios, we can see that **trade is beneficial to both countries if the terms of trade fall within the opportunity cost ratios**, that is to say if the price of 1 banana is somewhere between 2 apples and 3 apples. If a banana were to cost more than 3 apples, then Wilmania would be better off producing bananas itself; whereas if it cost less than 2 apples, then Fredonia would have no incentive to export bananas.

Let us suppose that on world markets 1 banana exchanges for 2.5 apples. We are assuming for the sake of argument that the terms of trade settle exactly half-way between the opportunity cost limits shown in Table 2. (In practice, the terms of trade can settle at any level, depending on world market conditions for the two products). Let us also suppose that Wilmania wants the same number of bananas as it had in Table 1. For these 3 bananas it will have to pay 7.5 apples.

The position after international trade is shown in Table 5. Wilmania has imported 3 bananas, leaving Fredonia with 7, and in exchange has exported 7.5 apples, keeping 10.5 for itself.

To see the **gains from trade** we must compare Table 5 with Table 1. Wilmania is clearly better off than before, since instead of 9 apples and 3 bananas it now has 10.5 apples and 3 bananas, so it is on balance 1.5 apples better off.

The position for Fredonia is not quite so clear. It has gained 2 bananas, but lost 2.5 apples. However, Table 2 shows us that before specialisation Fredonia's extra 2 bananas would have been worth 4 apples, so on balance Fredonia has gained by the equivalent of 4 − 2.5 = 1.5 apples. The end result of specialisation and trade is therefore that both countries are better off by the equivalent of 1.5 apples. In this example, both countries are equally better off, because the terms of trade happened to settle exactly halfway between the opportunity cost ratios. You can use simple numerical examples yourself to show how **the benefits of trade are distributed with different terms of trade ratios**, and how terms of trade outside these ratios would result in one country benefiting at the other's expense.

The above example makes a number of assumptions. For example, in reality, some of the benefits of trade are reduced by such things as **transport costs** and transactions costs such as the need to change currencies. On the other hand, the benefits might be increased by **economies of scale**, doubling the number of UPRs devoted to a product might actually more than double the output. And it is obvious that in reality there are not just two countries and two products in the world, but hundreds of countries and millions of products. This means that comparative advantages might in practice be very difficult to identify

The UK can produce oil more readily than France because it happens to have oil fields.

and calculate. Nevertheless, the above model is widely accepted in the modern world, and it would be very difficult to find an economist or politician who would deny that this helps to prove that on the whole international trade is a 'good thing'.

Competitive advantage

Why do countries import goods they can produce for themselves? The theory of comparative advantage is good at explaining why countries trade in order to obtain things they cannot produce for themselves. But why is it that Saudi Arabia, a desert country, imports sand? Why does Britain, with its North Sea resources, import oil? Why does so much trade take place between industrial manufacturing countries whose products, such as computers, machine tools and cars, are in many respects very similar to each other? Costs are important because of their effect on prices, but consumers are also influenced by such things as styling, quality, after-sales service, and powerful brand images created by persuasive advertising. Often we find that it is not a particular nation which has a comparative advantage, but a particular firm. In recent years the American economist Michael Porter has put forward the influential idea of **competitive advantage**. The basic idea is that competitive advantage is fostered by stiff competition between firms on their home market. This competition makes them efficient, as they concentrate on beating each other for price and quality, and this leaves firms well placed to compete abroad. As well as competition, there are important opportunities for cooperation between firms, especially between firms that supply each other (the 'supply chain' in the jargon). Firms build up networks with other firms, and benefit from the existence in the business environment of such things as transport infra-structures, financial institutions, and skilled human resources (in economics textbooks the topic of '**external economies**' is relevant to this idea). Similar firms can gather in specialised areas which become known for a certain type of business activity (the 'café quarter' in many large towns; or the famous and larger scale example of Silicon Valley in California). Regional Development Agencies in the UK are devoting a lot of resources towards encouraging automotive firms, electronics companies, and other industries perceived as being 'up-and-coming' to join forums which encourage them to think of themselves as 'clusters' which, it is hoped become focus points for economic growth. Many economists argue that it could be that *intelligent regions*, rather than nation states, will become increasingly important in the future as trading entities. Catalonia, in Spain, is often held up as a role model in this regard.

Multinational enterprises and intra-firm trade

With the growth of multinational enterprises, much trade crossing national boundaries is actually intra-firm trade; the Ford company, for example, exporting engines from Wales to its plant in Valencia. Many multinationals are becoming more monopolistic, as certain industries become dominated by fewer, larger firms. It is often difficult to identify whether a car, for instance, is domestically produced or imported. International trade theory depends very much on the idea of competition, but multinational firms are often very adept at operating anti-competitive practices. For example, they might indulge in **transfer pricing**, whereby a subsidiary company in one country will sell components to another part of the enterprise in another country at an artificial price. This might be an artificially low price, aimed at undercutting the competition. It might alternatively be an artificially high price, aimed at eliminating paper profits and so reducing the tax bill in a certain country.

National boundaries are also shifting. When the Soviet Union became eleven separate states in 1991, did the trade between those states suddenly change from being domestic to international? Now that Scotland has a separate parliament, should we begin to worry about the balance of payments of Scotland? For how much longer will people in the UK regard goods from France as 'imports', when both countries belong to the European Union? It could be that the change will come if or when Britain joins the single currency (the 'euro'). Or it could be argued that in an increasingly globalised world the change has already happened in practice.

How are comparative and competitive advantages created?

Why are some countries more efficient than others at producing certain goods and services? Firstly, this might be due to **natural factor endowments**, which are usually beyond the control of an individual country. The UK can produce oil more readily than France, simply because it happens to have oil fields which do not exist on French territory. Sometimes, a comparative advantage can last for a long time. France, for example, has produced wine for thousands of years. Recently, however, places like Latin America and Australia have combined technology with suitable climatic conditions to challenge that advantage.

Why did Japan emerge in the 1980s as a country that had become more efficient than the UK at car manufacturing? This is largely due to **past investment, both in capital equipment, and in people.** Japan had devoted resources towards building up its productive capacity, and in acquiring the knowledge and skills necessary to utilise that capacity efficiently. Within the general comparative advantage of the Japanese business environment, its companies built up their competitive advantage through innovative management techniques, which included 'lean production' techniques and 'just in time' supply chains.

Different countries might have different *attitudes* towards things such as long-term investment, education and training; they might have different *priorities*: they might, for instance prefer present consumption to investment in the future. It might be that the existence or otherwise of *institutions* makes a difference. Banks, trade unions, investment agencies and financial markets all have a part to play in economic development and so affect comparative and competitive advantage. American economists regard 'flexible labour markets' as an important source of competitive advantage. In effect, this means allowing employers the power to hire and fire their employees at will. European economists are more likely to speak of the need for *'flexible labour practices'*, an idea which involves employers and employees working in partnership to seek efficiency gains (see Chapter 5). The political background might also be important; businesses need political stability if they are to make long term investment, and the political institutions at the international, national and regional levels all have their important roles.

Chapter 3
What is happening to the UK balance of payments?

The international scene

Back in the late 1960s, the balance of payments was front page news on almost every day. Harold Wilson was the Labour prime minister at the time, and the low point of his administration occurred when the pound was devalued against other currencies. During the general election campaign of 1970 Edward Heath, the Conservative leader, struggled to convince the electorate that 'rising prices' presented a more important problem, and when Heath unexpectedly won the election the media were convinced that this was mainly due to 'bad trade figures'. Today, the pound fluctuates freely against other countries, devaluation or revaluation therefore happening every day and trade figures hardly figure in public consciousness at all.

Although it is possible to argue that unemployment has often been given insufficient attention, during recent decades **inflation** has usually been regarded as 'Public Enemy Number One'. Today, however inflation appears to be under control and indeed economists sometimes worry about moving towards a period of falling prices. When this has happened in Japan it has been associated with deflation (low or negative growth and rising unemployment). At times in the UK's past when prices have fallen – during the Great Depression of the 1930s, for example – our economic and social history has not been a particularly happy one. Falling prices might be an attractive idea to producers and exporters, but what if customers cannot afford to buy because they are either out of work or living in fear of unemployment?

The UK position

It has long been recognised that changes in the level of aggregate demand have an important influence on the UK balance of payments. The British people have a **high propensity to import** meaning that any increase in income results in expenditure on imported goods. Traditionally, an increase in aggregate demand leads to a balance of payments deficit and a sterling crisis, whereas a slowdown in the domestic economy generally results in a reduction in imports and so 'improves' the measured balance of payments. However, this has not been happening at the end of the 1990s and in recent years since the turn of the century. Contrary to what we would have expected from the UK's history of 'stop-go' the balance of payments has become a less sensitive indicator of the level of domestic activity in the UK. Whether the economy booms or is near recession and struggling to grow at all, we seem to always have deficits on our external trade and payments. Why is this? Partly it is because there has been a collapse in manufactured exports, and we are importing goods from places like India and China. However, these are not necessarily 'Indian' or 'Chinese' goods. In a sense they are 'British' because in common with businesses in other western nations, UK firms are researching, designing and developing their products in Britain, then contracting their manufacturing out to Chinese factories, then bringing the goods back for sale on UK markets. China is further discussed in Chapter 16.

The UK's economy has become more *stable* in terms of macroeconomic indicators such as the inflation rate, but at the same time *unbalanced* in terms of industrial sectors (this is further discussed in Chapter 4). Retailing, for example, is often described as 'booming', with foreign players in this market such as Wal-Mart of the USA eager to establish a foothold in this country (the Wal-Mart group now owns the Asda chain). Manufacturing, on the other hand, tends towards being more or less in constant recession, with output under pressure and (even more worryingly) future domestic investment plans severely curtailed.

There is also **regional imbalance**. During the recent 'boom' phases of the UK economy the financial and service-based economies of places like Camberley and Guildford were often regarded as 'overheating' and a large amount of attention was paid to the volatile state of the housing market in such places. However areas such as South West Wales and North East England which were more dependent on manufacturing and the export of goods were far more used to hearing bad news about actual or potential job losses.

Problems of manufacturing

Although as we noted in Chapter 1 manufacturing itself only accounts officially for about 20% of the UK economy, its actual significance is greater. The first reason for this is that a lot of activities that used to be carried out under the manufacturing 'umbrella' have now been contracted out. A factory might have had its own accountancy section, for example. These accountants were not in themselves manufacturers, but their jobs contributed to the manufacturing head-count. If this same factory now buys in its accountancy services, measured employment in the secondary sector now looks smaller, and tertiary (service-sector) employment looks larger, while in reality, in terms of numbers employed, little has really changed.

Another reason for the significance of manufacturing is that it supports large parts of the service sector. If manufacturing is in recession this feeds into a much larger proportion of the economy through such things as transport and financial services. It should also be remembered that a large amount, probably the majority, of research and development (R&D) takes place in the manufacturing sector. Politicians who say that they want a 'knowledge-based economy' at the same time as suggesting that manufacturing does not matter, are guilty of a lack of joined-up thinking.

Manufacturers have complained when the pound was regarded as **overvalued** against other major currencies. If there is a balance of payments deficit, we would expect importers to be offering sterling pounds for sale in exchange for foreign currencies in order to purchase their imports. Similarly, overseas traders would reduce their demand for the pound, as they purchase from other countries instead. An increase in the supply of pounds together with an increase in demand for other currencies would normally be expected to reduce the price (exchange rate) of the pound against other currencies. However, until the recession of 2008 relatively high interest rates in the UK (compared with other European countries) tended to attract foreign currencies into London money markets, and pull up the exchange rate of sterling. This in turn increased the overseas price of UK exports, and reduced the UK price of imported products, thus continuing the balance of payments deficit. During the recession that began in 2008 (see Chapter 17), the pound fell until it was close to parity with the euro. This was bad news for British tourists heading for the continent, and for British importers, but good news for British manufacturing exporters.

Balance of payments accounts

The balance of payments provides a summary of a country's international transactions over a given time period.

Figure 3.1: UK balance of payments, current account

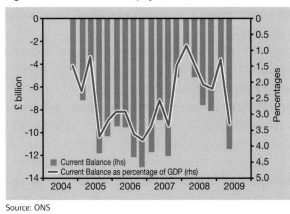

Source: ONS

Figure 3.1 shows some of trends in the UK balance of payments in recent years. The current account shows dealings in goods and services (international currency flows arising out of **consumption**). Another section shows **investment and financial accounts** (international currency flows arising out of long term movements of **capital**). A minus quantity indicates a currency outflow, while a positive amount indicates a flow of currency into the UK. Figures are 'seasonally adjusted'. Seasonal adjustment is necessary because of, for example, the effects of the seasons on the

harvesting of agricultural products, the closure of some sea routes in winter, and the reduced rate of trade in some industries during the summer holidays (with increased trade in other sectors, such as tourism). Seasonal adjustment uses an analysis of past data to remove any distortions due to purely seasonal factors.

Balance and equilibrium

In principle the overall balance of payments should balance by summing to zero. This is in line with what is called 'double entry book-keeping'. Every balance of payments entry should involve equal credit and debit entries showing monetary flows in opposite directions. For instance, the export of a machine from the UK to the USA would appear as a positive item in the current account, with payment in pounds for the machine flowing into the UK and being deposited in a British bank. At the same time, the transaction will be matched by a negative item or items. For example, if the American importer spends dollars to acquire sterling from a UK financial institution in order to purchase the machine, then at the time of that transaction the flow of pounds is outwards and therefore negative.

Accuracy of official statistics

If you go to a website such as that of the OECD, or nationmaster.com, and use a calculator to add up the balance of payments of every country on the planet, you will find that the world as a whole appears to have either a balance of payments surplus or deficit. Since one country's surplus is, in effect, another country's deficit, and since planet Earth does not yet have trading relations with Mars or Venus, this must throw some doubt on the accuracy of published trade figures generally!

Information on entries made in respect of each item of international trade is likely to come from at least two different sources (for example, from the traders themselves, from banks, or from the customs authorities) and there is scope for inaccuracies. There might be time delays causing different entries to appear in the accounts for different time periods; entries might be converted into sterling at different exchange rates; or it might be that the sophistication and reliability of accounting and recording procedures differ from country to country. In order to bring the total of all entries to zero, a **balancing item** is included to reflect human error and 'unspecified items' which affect the compilation of the accounts. At times over the last two decades the size of this balancing item in the UK statistics was large enough to cause the statisticians to seek ways of improving their accuracy and in recent years significant changes in the way in which balance of payments statistics are collected have been made.

Other official statistics have also been accused of inaccuracy. For example when returns were being collated for the census of 2001, local authorities were finding that thousands of people had disappeared from their population figures, and the missing numbers were significant enough to have serious affects on government funding for such things as new houses, schools and public sector wages and pensions. One theory was that people were simply not cooperating with the officers collecting census returns, or were deliberately giving false information (for example, there was an internet campaign, particularly popular among young people, to enter 'Jedi Knight' as a respondent's religion). This lack of cooperation can be traced back to the Poll Tax of the 1980s, when people disappeared from the electoral register in order to avoid paying the so-called 'Community Charge', and is possibly related to the legacy 'Council Tax'. But it is probably more generally related to a general feeling that governments are becoming too intrusive in their wish to collect information on people. As far as trade figures are concerned, wilful non-cooperation is less likely, but there are inherent practical difficulties, as mentioned above, in collecting accurate statistics. Yet it is surprising in the 21st Century to find that figures are still being questioned when, as mentioned above, it was as long ago as 1970 that a close general election result was at least partly affected by adverse trade figures (which looked more favourable when later corrected). It is not unknown for annual trade figures to contain an estimate of 'net errors and omissions' totalling several billion pounds. If it is possible for such huge amounts to 'go missing', it is reasonable to suggest that extreme caution should be exercised before

The balance of payments must always balance.

important economic and political decisions are taken in response to a single year's trade figures. The important conclusion is that one-off results need to be examined in the light of longer term trends.

Does the balance of payments really matter?

Since, as mentioned earlier, in accounting terms the balance of payments must always balance, how can the balance of payments of the UK be a 'problem'? In a nutshell, a problem arises if the balancing act puts a strain on the domestic economy. We should not assume that a deficit is 'bad' and a surplus is 'good', for reasons which are discussed later. Modern thinking tends to favour the concept of 'equilibrium' in the balance of payments, with manageable deficits being cancelled out by mild surpluses over a period of years. A balance of payments deficit is not regarded as 'chronic' unless it exceeds an acceptable percentage of GDP. Most commentators would regard British deficits of the late 1990s as operating within acceptable limits. However, while this might be true in terms of *totals*, the *composition* of the deficit might cause more concern in the way in which it impacts on certain industrial sectors or regions.

We do not worry about the balance of payments of Shropshire, and do not even bother to collect the statistics to calculate it. Therefore we might argue that the balance of payments 'problem' of the UK would not exist if we simply ignored it. However, Shropshire does not have its own separate currency, and its economy is integrated into a larger one (the economy of the UK). As the UK becomes more closely integrated into the 'single market' of the EU, then it can be argued that the balance of payments with Europe becomes less significant, and if or when the UK joins the euro, there comes a point when trade among Eurozone members becomes 'domestic' rather than 'international'. However, the Balance of Payments is important, to the extent that it creates monetary strains, and also affects the real economy. Monetary strains occur, for example, when one generation imports more than it exports, and so lives above its means leaving it to the next generation to repay the debts. Effects on the real economy are all too evident when jobs are lost in export industries; all too often these jobs are localised in areas which can least afford to lose them.

Chapter 4

How is trade affected by demand-side policy?

The background

In this chapter and the next we examine the linkages between domestic economic policy and Britain's external trading position.

Macroeconomic policy has changed considerably in recent years. In order to be able to comment critically on current macroeconomic policy it is necessary first to understand the main objectives and methods of traditional policy. 'Traditional' here refers to the way in which western governments tried to control their economies in the 30 years or so following the Second World War; that is, from the late 1940s to about 1980, when governments used '**Keynesian**' techniques, or policies influenced by the economist John Maynard Keynes. Following the credit crunch and recession of 2008, Keynesian demand management policies suddenly became fashionable once again (see Chapter 17).

Macroeconomic policy is sometimes referred to as 'stabilisation policy'. This is because it is recognised that the economy is affected by the booms and slumps of the business cycle, and that governments have a role in 'stabilising' or smoothing out the peaks and troughs of economic activity. A 'boom' (or 'recovery') occurs when an economy's output is growing, unemployment is falling and incomes are rising; a 'slump' (or 'recession') occurs when output is falling, unemployment is rising and incomes are falling.

The four main aims of stabilisation policy are usually given as: stable prices; balance of payments equilibrium, full employment, and steady growth.

Table 4.1: The traditional Keynesian 'grid'

Problem area	Monetary policy	Budgetary policy	Other possibilities
Inflation	Restrictive	Deflationary	Prices and incomes controls
Falling £ (Balance of payments deficits)	Restrictive	Deflationary	Import controls, devaluation
Rising £ (Balance of payments surpluses)	Expansive	Reflationary	Revaluation
Unemployment	Expansive	Reflationary	Incomes policy
Low Growth	Expansive	Reflationary	Remove controls

Stable prices are important for a country's competitiveness, and so are closely linked to the balance of payments. Full employment is closely linked to economic growth, since one is difficult to achieve without the other; and so it is possible to reduce these four 'problem areas' to two key issues: inflation and unemployment.

Various price indices are used to measure inflation. In the UK, the government publishes two versions of an index called the RPI (Retail Price Index): one is the headline inflation index which includes mortgage interest repayments, and the other is the underlying inflation index which does not do so. When interest rates are high, headline inflation is likely to be greater than underlying inflation; and vice versa when interest rates are low. In recent years, the Consumer Prices Index (CPI) has been adopted by the UK government as its official inflation rate. This essentially uses the same methods of collecting information on a 'basket' of goods and services as is used throughout the EU. This index is weighted towards items that are widely purchased across the whole of the EU, and this means in practice that it contains a high proportion of products that are actually falling in price in real terms: electronic goods, computers, mobile phones and the like. Thus the CPI tends to give a lower 'reading' for inflation than the RPI. The official inflation rate has been criticised for this reason. Senior citizens, for example, complain that it does not give a realistic picture of increases in their cost of living, since they tend to spend more on such things as home heating, and energy prices have been rising faster than other items. The CPI does not, at the moment, contain an element reflecting the cost of housing, and has been criticised for this reason also.

Until recently, the UK government has used the **claimant count** measure, that is those people claiming unemployment benefit are defined as the unemployed. An obvious problem with this is that the unemployment total can be reduced simply by making it more difficult to claim. Now (since spring 1998), the UK government uses the **International Labour Organisation (or ILO) method** of counting which is a sample survey that identifies those of working age and those seeking work. This method is used by most countries.

When considering the effects of inflation and unemployment, a useful technique is to view these problems from different viewpoints: for instance employers, employees, producers, consumers, exporters, importers, government, taxpayer, lender, borrower, savers. Very often, what is 'bad news' for one, is 'good news' for another. Inflation, for example, is bad news for savers, or for pensioners and students (on low, fixed incomes), but may be good news for property-owners and borrowers. So the question is: do we want society to encourage saving or borrowing? Unemployment might be bad news for employees, but good news for employers (if they can offer lower wages); on the other hand, low wages lead to low demand, so employers in their role as producers/sellers, might find unemployment very bad news indeed.

Table 4.2: Components of aggregate demand, UK, 2008

Component	Amount (£bn)
Consumption	927
Government spending	313
Investment	246
Exports (net of imports)	-38
Total (Gross Domestic Product at market prices)	1448

Source: ONS, *National Income 'Blue Book'*, 2009
(This total does not include an estimate for statistical errors)

Until the end of the 1970s, the policies which governments used to achieve their objectives were known as **demand management techniques**. These are essentially short-run techniques. They take the 'supply side' conditions of the economy such as its productive capacity as being given, and they attempt to increase employment or reduce inflation by increasing or decreasing total demand in the economy. Total demand in the economy is known as 'aggregate demand (AD)'.

In round figures, the value of total AD (and therefore national income) for the UK is nearly £1,500 billion as shown in Table 4.2. On this measure the UK economy is one of the largest in the world.

Aggregate demand can be increased or decreased in two broad ways: through monetary policy and through fiscal policy.

Monetary policy affects the supply of money in the economy by influencing the amount of lending by banks and other institutions, and also the price of credit, or the interest rate. A 'restrictive' monetary policy consists of credit controls and high interest rates. An 'expansive' monetary policy consists of easy credit and low interest rates;

Fiscal policy, sometimes known as budgetary policy, affects demand by working on taxation and government spending. A 'deflationary' budgetary policy consists of lower government spending and higher taxes. Higher taxes reduce people's disposable incomes, and therefore reduce consumer demand. A

'reflationary' budgetary policy consists of higher government spending and lower taxes. Lower taxes increase people's disposable incomes and therefore increase consumer demand.

Traditional stabilisation policy used monetary policy to set the scene, or to establish the general atmosphere (restrictive, discouraging spending or expansive, encouraging spending). Budgetary policy was then used to 'fine tune' the economy, that is to attempt to hit particular inflation or employment targets with either a 'deflationary' or 'reflationary' budget.

An important problem with 'reflationary' budgets is that they can also be 'inflationary'. With higher government spending at the same time as lower taxation, there might be a budget deficit. Critics of deficit financing, as it is called, accuse governments of causing inflation by in effect 'printing money' to cover their budget deficits.

In recent years the objectives of government policy changed, and so did government priorities. Whereas it used to be thought that the government's first priority should be to tackle unemployment, now inflation has become an over-riding concern, and it is widely believed that tackling inflation in the first instance would lead eventually to the solving of other problems.

There developed a much greater stress on **the supply side** of the economy. A major problem with trying to influence short-run demand is that objectives can conflict. For example, lower unemployment might lead to increased inflation. This could occur for 'demand-pull' or 'cost-push' reasons. From a demand point of view, lower unemployment leads to higher incomes, which in turn could pull up prices if there are bottlenecks in the supply of goods and services. From a cost point of view, lower unemployment might make wage negotiators more 'pushy' on behalf of the workforce, thus pushing up wage costs, which might be passed on in higher prices. This possible conflict between full employment and low inflation is known as a policy 'trade-off', and is illustrated in most textbooks by means of the 'Phillips Curve'.

Figure 4.1: Internal and external balance

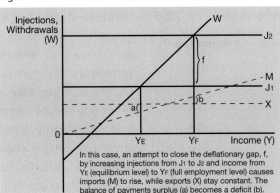

In this case, an attempt to close the deflationary gap, f, by increasing injections from J₁ to J₂ and income from Yᴇ (equilibrium level) to Yꜰ (full employment level) causes imports (M) to rise, while exports (X) stay constant. The balance of payments surplus (a) becomes a deficit (b).

Another trade-off is between the 'internal' and 'external' economy. Full employment at home will lead to higher incomes; however if there is a tendency to import luxury goods (as there is in the UK) higher incomes can lead to balance of payments difficulties. This has been a major cause of the 'stop-go policies' that Britain has traditionally suffered from, or as politicians tend to say nowadays: *'boom and bust'*.

Unemployment after the Second World War was dramatically lower than before 1939, and consistently low for three decades afterwards. However, Keynesian policies depend on the idea of a 'trade off'. During the early 1970s, there was high unemployment, high inflation, record balance of payments deficits, and low growth, all at the same time. This was largely due to the 'external shock' caused by the decision of the oil producing countries to increase the price of oil. This external shock was both inflationary and deflationary at the same time. How could this be so? The shock was inflationary, in that it pushed up prices, because the western world's dependence on oil for transport, energy generation and in its chemical industries increased the costs of production. At the same time the shock was deflationary, because it created unemployment, when employers attempted to reduce costs by 'shaking out' what they saw as surplus staff. This unemployment in turn reduced incomes and therefore reduced demand and led to recession.

As mentioned above, the traditional Keynesian view of the economy was that macroeconomic policy could be used to influence aggregate demand. A reduction in aggregate demand would reduce inflation, and also reduce balance-of-payments deficits. An increase in aggregate demand would stimulate growth and employment; it might, however, bring about some inflationary tendencies, or encourage imports which would have to be paid for somehow, perhaps through borrowing if there were insufficient reserves of foreign currency. As long as politicians could manage a 'trade-off' between objectives, then all was well, but the oil price hike of the early 1970s meant that all the major policy areas appeared to be failing at once. Many economists were attracted to the 'monetarist' ideas of Milton Friedman of the University of Chicago. What were the main tenets of Keynesians and monetarists and what did these tenets mean?

Table 4.3: Basic principles of Keynesians and monetarists (neo-classical)

KEYNESIANS	MONETARISTS
1. Employment and output depend on aggregate demand	1. Employment and output depend on supply side factors
2. Unregulated free markets do not work: they are unstable; unsocialised markets are a threat to freedom	2. Markets work; over-mighty governments are a threat to freedom
3. Governments need to regulate aggregate demand to achieve full employment	3. Governments harm the economy if they intervene
4. Governments can use a multiplier effect	4. Government investment 'crowds out' private investment
5. There is a 'trade-off' between inflation and unemployment, and full employment is more important than low inflation	5. In the long run, inflation causes unemployment; and low inflation is more important than full employment
6. Money does not matter	6. Money is all that matters

Aggregate demand, or total demand in the whole economy, is made up of four main parts or components. Firstly, consumption, that is the demand by households for everyday goods and services. Secondly, investment or the demand by firms for capital goods such as machinery, buildings, vehicles and so on. Thirdly, the government adds to aggregate demand by public spending, or the government's purchasing of goods and services. Fourthly, there is net demand from overseas trade: the demand from people in other countries for the home country's exports, minus the home country's demand for imported goods and services.

Keynesians argue that free markets will not, by themselves, ensure that the level of aggregate demand in the economy will be sufficient to produce the amount of output that is necessary for full employment. Left to its own devices, aggregate demand may be higher or lower than the full employment level. Therefore, government intervention is needed to alter aggregate demand.

In the post-war period, the use of Keynesian policies by western governments produced full employment; however Keynes had little to say about the problem of inflation. The main theory which Keynesians adopted in order to explain why inflation occurred was known as the Phillips Curve.

Figure 4.2: A 'Phillips Curve' trade-off

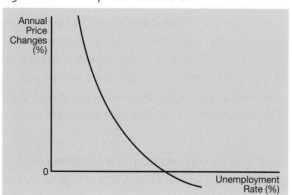

The Phillips Curve was developed by Professor A.W. Phillips of the London School of Economics. He studied statistics which showed that over much of the Twentieth Century there was a close **inverse relationship between changes in wage rates and the level of unemployment**. Since wage rates can be assumed to be linked to prices, this has been taken by many economists to mean that there is a 'trade-off' between inflation and unemployment. During periods when inflation is high, unemployment tends

What is the relationship between money supply and inflation?

to be low, and vice versa. When unemployment is very high indeed, inflation is low, and might even be negative, with prices falling. Figure 4.2 illustrates the Phillips Curve concept. There are two main ways of explaining this apparent relationship. Firstly, a demand-pull explanation. When unemployment is high, earnings are low and therefore demand is low. This reduces demand-pull inflation. Secondly, a cost-push explanation. When unemployment is high, trade unions feel that jobs are insecure and are therefore less 'pushy' when making wage claims. This tends to reduce inflationary pressure from wage costs.

As far as the supply of money is concerned, Keynes himself believed that the supply of money had little if anything to do with the amount of money in circulation. However modern Keynesians are more reluctant to totally dismiss the importance of the money stock.

On the other hand monetarists believe that there is a close relationship between the money supply and inflation. An increase in the rate of growth of the supply of money will lead to higher inflation rates; a fall in the rate of growth of the supply of money will slow down inflation.

While Keynesians believed that output depends on demand, monetarists believed that 'supply creates its own demand', and the volume of output therefore depends on supply side factors, or the ability of producers to create the goods and services that consumers want. They argued that market forces, if left to themselves, are the most efficient way of deciding on what to produce. Furthermore, they believed that labour is bought and sold on a market, and that provided the 'price' of labour (the wage rate) is allowed to find its own level, markets will achieve full employment. Impediments to the functioning of labour markets mean that zero unemployment is unlikely, as there is such a thing as a **natural rate of unemployment** caused by such issues as minimum wage laws and trade union activities. Government intervention aimed at reducing unemployment below its natural rate will not work and might simply cause inflation in the short term and even higher levels of unemployment in the long term.

Monetarists denied that there is any trade-off between inflation and unemployment in the long run; indeed the monetarist view is that inflation is an important cause of unemployment. Milton Friedman, who was regarded as the father of monetarism, argued that there is little in practice that governments can do about output and unemployment levels, but since governments are responsible for the money supply they can control inflation by reducing the rate of growth of the supply of money. In effect, this means that governments should reduce their own spending and reduce their economic activity. Monetarism therefore has special appeal to politicians from the 'right wing' of the political spectrum, as they can be expected to be in favour of reduced government involvement in the economy. According to Friedman the money supply is the sole determinant of the one variable that governments are able to control in the long run: the rate of inflation.

In practice, governments in the 1980s found it very difficult to control the supply of money. Monetary targets laid down by the government were regularly exceeded. During the 1980s, the de-regulation of the financial markets, and the globalisation of the banking system, together with the growth of plastic payment cards and electronic transfers made it very difficult for traditional controls to work. Governments found that they could influence the 'price' of money (the interest rate) to some extent, but they could not control the actual supply. Monetarism, in its narrow sense, as a technique for controlling inflation by controlling the supply of money, has been abandoned. However, 'monetarism' in its wider sense, encompassing the Thatcherite 'supply-side' policies, was very much in the ascendancy, and is still influential today. In the past, differences between Keynesians and Monetarists were essentially differences over factual evidence as to which theories of inflation and employment worked best. Today, there is a larger measure of agreement over policies, and there is a new stress by all economists on the supply-side.

Where today's descendants of the Keynesians and Monetarists differ is largely on their view of the role of the state, on the way in which society should be organised, on income distribution, and on whether it is 'right' or 'wrong' for certain functions of the government, such as the provision of a welfare state, to be privatised, In other words, it is a *normative debate* reflecting the type of society we wish to live in, rather than a technical debate about objective economic mechanisms.

To sum up then, the four traditional objectives of macroeconomic policy are: stable prices, full employment, steady growth and balance of payments equilibrium. In Keynesian thinking, monetary policy sets the scene, either expansionary or restrictive, through interest rates and credit controls; budgetary or fiscal policy 'fine tunes' the economy, achieving either reflation or deflation through adjustments in public spending and direct and indirect taxation.

Macroeconomic policy today

In the late 1990s a new economic orthodoxy swept the world. Politicians, government advisers, international institutions, and business analysts are now using a model of the economy which is neither purely 'Monetarist' or 'Keynesian,' but contains elements of both these world-views, together with some internal inconsistencies.

In recent years, governments have changed their views on both the range of objectives that can be achieved through pulling macroeconomic levers, and on the types of levers themselves.

In normal times in recent years there has been a much greater stress on **balanced budgets**, with governments reluctant to alter taxes, especially income taxes. Fiscal or budgetary policy attempts to be 'rules-based'. Gordon Brown, as Chancellor of the Exchequer, introduced his 'golden rule' and 'sustainable investment' rule which taken together added up to a commitment to balance budgets over a medium term time period, and to avoid public sector borrowing unless it is for investment with a return. However, these rules were dropped as a reaction to the financial crises and massive government borrowing that emerged in 2008, and it remains to be seen whether recovery will be quick or strong enough to allow their re-instatement in the near future. Up until 2008, modern demand management focused almost entirely on the 'single golf club' of the interest rate. Post 2008, additional measures such as 'quantitative easing' and 'fiscal boost' have been taken on board by the UK and other major economies (see Chapter 17).

Up to 2008, short-term anti-cyclical policy was perceived to be demand-led. This was a Keynesian perception. Then a monetary instrument, the 'single golf club' of the interest rate was used to influence

demand. This was basically a Monetarist policy. In the long-run supply-side policies are used to reduce the non-inflationary level of unemployment. These policies include a mix of monetarist/neo-classical prescriptions, for example flexible labour markets and welfare to work. Some supply side policies are more Keynesian in tone such as monopoly regulation, education and training, private/public partnerships for investment in infrastructure and public services).

Governments meanwhile believe that they have to take special care to convince multinational enterprises, international institutions and global markets that they are serious about reducing inflationary expectations by pursuing 'sound' economic management. Essentially this involves attempting to reduce government borrowing, taxation and hence public expenditure, as prescribed in the IMF/World Bank world view, the EU's Maastricht criteria and the Eurozone's convergence rules, all of which, as already mentioned, have been seriously undermined by the financial crises of 2007/8 (see Chapter 17).

Shortly after becoming Chancellor of the Exchequer in 1997, Gordon Brown handed responsibility for setting interest rates to the Monetary Policy Committee (MPC) of the Bank of England. The MPC's brief was to target underlying RPI inflation at a level of 2.5% (with a 1 percentage point margin above or below). The target was later changed to be 2% on the CPI measure. In order to achieve this target, the MPC has to consider various economic indicators (see Table 4.3).

Table 4.3: Selected economic indicators, November 2009

Output	(Figures below show annual percentage changes)
GDP	-0.3
Manufacturing output	-10.9
Service industry	-0.2
Goods exports, volume	-12.8
Demand	
Household consumption	-0.7
Retail sales	0.4
Whole economy investment	-11.4
Business investment	-21.7
Goods imports, volume	-13.5
Inflation rates	
Headline (RPI, retail price index)	0.3
Underlying (RPIX, excludes mortgage interest payments)	2.7
CPI (Consumer Prices Index, EU measure of inflation, targeted by Bank of England	1.9
Unemployment	2.49 million (7.9%) (Labour Force Survey)
Exchange rate index	
1990	100
November 1995	82.2 (Lowest during Conservative government)
June 1997	97.2 (Labour wins election)
May 2000	113.6 (Highest in recent years)
November 2009	80.4
Public sector debt	48.9% of GDP
Public sector net current borrowing	£77.3bn
Bank rate	0.5%

Source: Treasury website, www.hm-treasury.gov.uk, 15 December 2009

These indicators can be regarded as relating to four essential areas:

1. the real economy
2. inflation trends
3. monetary policy
4. external factors.

We shall examine these four aspects in turn.

1. An important concept in the 'real' economy is the **output gap**. This can be simply understood as relating to 'spare capacity' and is closely linked to the Keynesian idea of deflationary/inflationary gaps. It is also linked to monetarist/neo-classical ideas such as 'natural rate' or **the non-accelerating inflation rate of unemployment** or **'NAIRU'**. Whereas Keynesians compare actual output with potential output (to determine the size of 'inflationary' or 'deflationary' gaps), current orthodoxy measures output gaps by comparing actual output with 'sustainable' that is, non-inflationary output. The latter is shown as a 'trend growth' line. It is believed that in this country a growth rate of somewhere between 2 and 3% per annum is sustainable without excessive inflation. Figure 4.3 shows two ways of visualising the output gap: the vertical lines a and b in diagram (a) correspond closely to the horizontal line in diagram (b). The purpose of demand management policy can be regarded as reducing the peaks and troughs of the business cycle (in diagram a) or shifting the Aggregate Demand line (in diagram b) in order to reduce the size of the output gap. The purpose of supply-side policy (discussed in Chapter 5) can be regarded as that of shifting the horizontal line upwards (in diagram a), or shifting the Long Run Aggregate Supply curve to the right (diagram b), so that higher levels of output can coexist with lower levels of inflation.

Figure 4.3

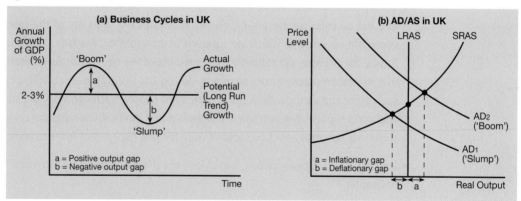

2. Where there is a negative output gap, or growth below the trend line, this more or less corresponds to what Keynesians call a **deflationary gap**. However, it is believed that there may be inflationary trends even with spare capacity, depending on the actual amount of spare capacity, the speed with which the output gap is being closed, and the extent to which spare capacity is usable, given such things as skills shortages. When there is a positive output gap, or growth above the trend line, we have a situation similar to Keynesian 'demand-pull inflation', where inflation is affected by likelihood of supply 'bottlenecks' and the ability or otherwise of imports to supply the demand.

3. The main monetary policy is the interest rate. Throughout the world control is increasingly being delegated to central bankers. Interest rates are used to control effective demand. In the UK, the burden of high interest rates falls to a large extent on variable-rate mortgage payers. There are far fewer variable-rate mortgagee payers than there are taxpayers, so it could be argued that this policy is less effective and also less equitable than using fiscal policy. It might be more effective if disposable income were to be reduced using progressive taxation rather than interest rates, since the effects would be felt more quickly and the response would be more *elastic*. An additional consideration is that the money

raised would then be available for government spending on economic and social priorities, rather than comprising windfall profits to banks and building societies. Taxes are also more equitable, that is to say fairer, since the pain can be shared amongst a wider section of the population rather than punishing mortgage payers for something they cannot help doing: living in their own houses.

In business terms, interest rates are a cost, due to the simple fact that a sizeable proportion of capital investment in industry takes place using borrowed money. High interest rates therefore make it more difficult for firms to so something which they must do in order to remain competitive: that is, to re-equip themselves. In the past, commentators as diverse as the Trades Union Congress and the Confederation of British Industry have claimed that high interest rates actually cause inflation. Many years ago Keynes argued strongly against the use of interest rates to influence the level of economic activity; however, due to a wide range of factors which are as much political as economic, current policy focuses on this single instrument almost to the exclusion of others.

4. External factors include:
    * Firstly, the pound sterling: if the pound is strong, this reduces input prices, and so assists in lowering inflation; however, it also hits exports, particularly of manufactures. This is discussed in Chapter 6.

    * Secondly, overseas influences such as the possibility of a downturn in the United States economy, where commentators are increasingly concerned about the possibility of a stock market 'correction' being necessary, due to inflated share prices largely caused by energetic dealing on internet shares where prices have tended to be unrealistically high in relation to profits. An overseas influence which is both beneficial and problematic is that of cheap goods from China. On the one hand they undermine manufacturing employment in the west but on the other hand they reduce inflation in the importing countries.

    * Thirdly there is the effect of commodity prices, particularly oil prices which are important to Britain as a net oil importer. Recent experience illustrates the volatility of the supply and price of these commodities, many of which are supplied in monopolistic markets. Countries importing gas from Russia, for example, are seriously concerned about the geo-political and economic aspects of being over-reliant on supplies from a country lacking the institutions that enable traders to have trust in each other and confidence in the continuity of supply. Such concerns will increase as time goes on and world supplies run out. Many economists and political scientists are convinced that history will show that concerns about oil supplies were the real reason that America went to war in Iraq.

    * Fourthly, the European context, particularly the effects of the single currency. This is further discussed in Chapter 7.

Issues arising from the new economic paradigm

Let us summarise some of the main issues arise from the current economic orthodoxy. There is no doubt that where interest rates targeting takes place, and independent central banks are given control of the interest rate in order to meet those targets, the results have proved to be impressive. However, it could be argued that there needs to be further debate about some of the spin-offs and side effects.

1. Firstly, some consideration needs to given to the issue of whether interest rate policy is more appropriate than other demand management techniques, such as progressive taxation. High interest rates affect the disposable incomes of consumers by increasing their monthly mortgage payments. However, it is a perhaps surprising fact that most houses in this country do not have a mortgage attached to them. Most houses are already paid for. Of the remainder, many householders have opted for fixed-rate mortgages, and so are immune to short-term interest rate variations. This tends to reduce the effect of anti-inflationary increases in interest rates, and means that interest rates have to be increased quite substantially before they take effect. Substantial increases have unfortunate side-effects. They cause

severe problems to people on a tight budget, by increasing their housing costs (house repossessions by building societies of homes whose occupants cannot keep up repayments have soared in recent years). High interest rates also add to industrial costs. As mentioned above, if a reduction in spending power is needed it might be more efficient, more effective, and also more fair and just if the 'misery' were more widely spread, through increases in progressive income tax.

2. Secondly, it needs to be asked whether high interest rates reduce or increase inflationary pressure. High interest rates work on borrowers, such as people with mortgages, to reduce demand by reducing disposable income. However, as argued earlier, they also increase industrial costs. However most of the economists with any influence in government circles would probably argue that on balance, in the long run, interest rates can be used successfully to squeeze inflationary expectations out of the economy. The results of the activities of the Monetary Policy Committee certainly point to the conclusion that within its own terms of reference, it has been successful. However, critics argue that it should take less notice of the distorting effects of the housing market in the south east, and perhaps that it should even be given employment and/or economic growth targets to aim at alongside its inflation target. Is an interest rate policy influenced by the overheated South East of England suitable for the less prosperous regions of Britain?

3. Thirdly, the question arises as to whether 'trend growth' is necessarily the same thing as 'sustainable growth'. Many economists, possibly including some members of the Bank of England's Monetary Policy Committee take the view that in a service-based high-technology economy higher levels of growth can exist with lower levels of inflation than in a goods-based economy.

4. Fourthly, there needs to be further debate about whether a 'pool' of unemployed people is a necessary condition for low inflation. The idea of *NAIRU* (or a non-accelerating inflation rate of unemployment) would certainly seem to be inconsistent with the UK government's 'welfare to work' policies. In recent years it is arguable that in place of a NAIRU, government policy has been based on a **'NAIRLWE' – a non-accelerating inflation rate of low-wage employment**. Rather than deliberately manage a 'pool' of unemployed, it has been possible to keep inflation within acceptable limits while moving very close towards full employment due to the existence of a pool of workers who are willing to work at or just above the **national minimum wage**. This wage level remains unattractive to many British people, who might find that the loss of benefits actually makes them worse off if they move from welfare to work. But this is not the case for many thousands of migrant workers, including a substantial number from the newer EU member countries, who are not entitled to the majority of UK welfare benefits, and to whom the British minimum wage is significantly higher than the wage rates they could expect back in their home country.

As far as the regions of the UK economy is concerned, it should be remembered that the country's long-run trend rate of growth of between 2 and 3% is an *average*. A monetary policy suitable for South East England is not necessarily appropriate for the regions, and dooms them to growth rates that are even lower. It has to be asked: if 2-3% is the best we can do, then what have all the supply-side changes (discussed later) actually achieved? Unless they enable us to move above the trend growth line, the answer to this question might be 'not a lot'. Meanwhile, interest rates aimed at keeping UK economy as whole on this trend growth line have serious effects for those sectors and regions particularly dependent on international trade.

In a nutshell, then, inflation in the short term is seen as being caused by demand diverging from trend growth. Interest rates are used as the main demand-management policy. In the long term, trend growth is thought to be amenable to improvement through supply-side measures (discussed in the next chapter). Britain's international trade is crucially affected by both sets of policies. Demand management policies affect the relative prices of export and imports in the short term; supply-side policies affect UK competitiveness on world markets in the longer term.

Chapter 5

How is trade affected by supply-side policy?

UK trade and supply-side policy

In the year 1850, the UK had 41 per cent of world trade in manufactures. This fell to 14 per cent by 1960, 9 per cent in 1970, and around 5 per cent in 2010. In 1945, the UK had the third highest GDP per head among industrialised nations. But by 1991 the country had slipped to fourteenth place, and during the 1990s it lost ground to rapidly growing countries like Ireland and even Spain. Now, in the second decade of the third millennium, the 'workshop of the world' is certainly not Britain, nor is it anywhere in Europe. China currently stakes the strongest claim to that title, with India not far behind.

For over 100 years governments of different political complexions have come and gone, but UK growth rates have persistently hovered at averages of 2-3% per year, while many competitors have done better. Politicians have continually bemoaned 'skills shortages' and economists regularly claim that the UK has failed to invest in either physical capital, through investment in technology, or human capital through investment in education. Only when there is a cultural change in the UK, so that resources are switched from spending to saving, from consumption to investment, will Britain achieve the competitiveness that is necessary to avoid long economic difficulties. Competitiveness and productivity are likely to be *the* two economic key-words of the next few years.

Figure 5.1: Unit wage costs

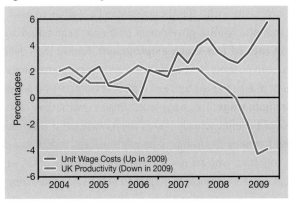

How can we measure the competitiveness of the UK? There is no single measure. However, one useful indicator is the concept of Unit Labour Costs This is calculated by dividing average output per worker into total labour costs and is shown in Figure 5.1.

As well as measures within the economy, such as investment in new technology and skills, competitiveness depends on the exchange rate. Domestic gains in productivity can be thwarted by adverse movements in the exchange rate index, which govern **relative unit labour costs**, or **international competitiveness**. Generally speaking, during the early 1980s, UK competitiveness improved until about 1989, and then grew worse until 1992. This was not helped by the fact that Britain's oil exports pulled up the value of the pound, which had the affect of making UK manufactured products appear expensive on overseas markets. The decline in competitiveness was reversed when Britain left the European Exchange Rate Mechanism and the pound devalued. Then competitiveness increased until the mid-1990s, when high interest rates and a strong pound began to have seriously adverse effects.

Output per worker measures the efficiency of a major industrial input (labour). Countries like Japan and West Germany, whose industries were devastated by World War II were forced to suffer a lower level of consumption than the UK in the early 1950s while they invested in new machinery and equipment. However, by the 1960s these countries were reaping the rewards, while Britain with its older industrial infrastructure was hard placed to compete. On international markets, the foreign exchange rate has an important effect on competitiveness. A strong pound increases the overseas price of exports, and reduces the UK price of imported goods (however, it also makes imported raw materials and components appear cheaper). A weak pound has the opposite effects.

Tony Blair put his faith in 'education, education and education' as a cure for our economic ills.

A major weakness in the UK is its **short termism** and lack of investment. Supply bottlenecks which help cause inflation and suck in imports will continue to be a problem if investment is inadequate. The UK has not re-equipped itself either in the sense of investment in plant and equipment, nor in the sense of investing in people at the educational level. As long ago as 1851, when Prince Albert promoted the Great Exhibition at Crystal Palace, British industrialists were shocked to discover the extent to which their technologies were falling behind those of other countries, particularly Germany at that time. Prime Minister William Gladstone later initiated an enquiry into the education system to try to discover whether changes could improve the UK's economic performance. Since then, Britain's decline through the economic league tables has been an issue at every general election. Former Prime Minister Tony Blair's faith in 'education, education and education' as a cure for our economic ills showed that times had not changed that much. UK trade policy continues to focus on the issue of 'competitiveness', and measures to improve Britain's competitive position figure large in policy statements.

One change of the last few years is a new stress on long term measures. It has been a feeling among some economists and politicians that demand management techniques may be all very well in the short run, but that at best they are irrelevant to the long run, and at worst they might actually be damaging. There has been a new stress on what are called **supply side policies** as a way of restructuring economies for the long run. During the 1980s the phrase 'supply side' was more or less hijacked by what might be termed the 'right wing', and so supply-side policies were at that time closely identified with the politics of Margaret Thatcher and Ronald Reagan.

Supply side policies can be defined in general terms as policies which are intended to increase the productive efficiency of the economy. Some of these policies can be regarded as 'free market' policies; others depend on more rather than less government intervention.

We now identify four aspects of free market supply side policies.

1. **Flexible labour markets.** During the Conservative government of 1979 to 1997, a series of anti-trade union laws were passed, designed to make it easier for employers to hire and fire staff. The result was a rapid expansion in short-term contracts, part-time working, the feminisation of the workforce (more

women in work than ever before), with a massive reduction in trade union membership. From one point of view this made the British workforce more 'flexible'. However, there are human and social costs associated with this policy. Many social analysts believe that when people are uncertain about their jobs this leads to stresses in society, leading to illness and social problems such as the break-up of families. It can also be economically dysfunctional, because if 'consumer confidence' or the often quoted 'feel good factor' is low, then this can lead to depressed demand. Firms which therefore benefit as employers, because they can employ cheaper workers, might be hit as producers from another direction by workers in their role as consumers.

2. **Tax and public spending reductions.** Free market supply siders believe that public spending is damaging because it merely 'crowds out' private spending. They also believe that income taxes act as a disincentive to hard work and enterprise. They therefore advocate tax reductions. This ideas has become so ingrained in the consciousness of many politicians that it has become very difficult for them to accept that taxation is a viable option, even to finance essentials such as health services and long-term pension funds.

3. **De-regulation.** Ironically, as the government in the 1980s was attempting to control the money supply, it was also de-regulating many branches of industry, including the banks. These policies were in tension with each other. As building societies were allowed to compete with commercial banks, and as international controls on banking activity were swept away, it became impossible for governments to control the supply of 'money' in its widest sense. This meant that monetarism, in the sense of attempting to control the growth of the money supply was no longer a viable policy. However 'monetarism' in the sense of supporting free-market friendly policies continued to dominate the political agenda.

4. **Privatisation.** Throughout the 1980s and early 1990s, assets which had been in public ownership were sold off by the state to the private sector. Telephones, gas, steel, electricity, water and railways were among the significant privatisations. This action raised revenue which the government used to finance tax reductions. It was argued that privatisation would increase efficiency and encourage competition. However many of the 'utilities' formed privatised monopolies, and because of the danger of monopoly power, they were supervised by 'regulators', part of whose brief was to protect consumer interests. The growth of these regulators is clearly in tension with the policy of de-regulation mentioned earlier.

The above are generally regarded as the 'Thatcherite' supply-side policies. They are geared towards freeing up markets and reducing government involvement in the economy. As explained in Chapter 4, Thatcherism was also very closely linked to 'Monetarism'. This involved control of the money supply in the belief that this would control inflation. However the control of the money supply is not usually regarded in itself as being strictly speaking a 'supply side' policy as such, as it is not directly related to measures aimed at increasing output or productivity. However, monetarists believe that governments are guilty of encouraging lending and borrowing, and so control of the money supply naturally leads to attempts to control government borrowing, and therefore government spending. Thatcherite politicians might argue that reducing government intervention will increase business efficiency in the long run. Keynesian or neo-Keynesian economists, on the other hand, might well argue that it is the type of government intervention that is crucial, and that some types of public spending (on transport infrastructure, for example) have direct effects on private sector efficiency and output levels.

Keynesian or neo-Keynesian economists would be likely to argue with the desirability of the free-market supply side policies discussed above, but are by no means opposed to all measures aimed at improving the supply side. (Keynes himself regarded the supply side of the economy as crucial, but in the long run rather than the short run). New Labour's 'Third Way' involved (as far as we could tell) the acceptance of many Thatcherite policies, such as privatisation, but superimposed several policies that could be described as 'new' or 'neo' Keynesian, especially a declared commitment towards education and training. However, there was still room left for much debate: for example on the difference between 'flexible labour markets' (favoured in the UK and USA) and 'flexible working practices (favoured in continental Europe and Scandinavia).

It was never exactly clear what New Labour politicians meant when they spoke of the 'Third Way'. Presumably this phrase drew attention to the idea that policies were neither Thatcherite nor did they signal a return to nationalisation and massive government intervention. What we could see, in concrete terms, was a continued stress on the supply-side, but with rather a different emphasis, particularly with respect to the following policies.

1. **An anti-monopoly, pro-competition policy.** British competition policy has often been criticised for being weak and inconsistent compared with, say, American 'anti-trust' laws. But there have been recent changes in the administration of UK policy that are more reassuring. The 2002 Enterprise Act established the Office of Fair Trading (OFT) as an independent statutory body. Under the Act the OFT and the Competition Commission now have the final say over whether mergers are anti-competitive or not. The role of the Secretary of State is substantially reduced. The introduction of 'a substantial lessening of competition' test brings UK policy close to that in the US. The 2002 Enterprise Act has helped to depoliticise UK competition policy.

2. **The existence of public/private partnerships.** These are aimed at providing new infrastructure without relying as much as in the past on using tax revenues: the building of a toll motorway north of Birmingham is an example. They are also aimed at bringing private sector money into the public sector: the involvement of private enterprise in the so-called 'education action zones' is an example. These measures are controversial, to say the least.

3. **A new stress on education and training.** The catchphrase 'education, education and education' is symbolically important, even if it remains to be translated into real spending priorities and actual achievements.

4. **A more 'European' outlook on supply side issues.** For example the UK has adopted Europe-wide agreements on aspects of working conditions, such as employment protection and working hours.

5. **A movement towards flexible working practices.** These are not quite the same thing as flexible labour markets. Flexible labour markets are essentially anti-trade union and pro-employer; they increase uncertainty and give employers the right to hire and fire. Flexible working practices involve such things as multi-tasking (where, for example the 'demarcation' lines between one group of workers and another are removed, so reducing the inefficiencies when plumbers, for instance were not allowed to do a job reserved for electricians. Flexible working practices depend to a large extent on co-operation with trade unions rather than their elimination, and on a new attitude from the more enlightened unions who realise that re-training for multi-tasking is in the long-term interest of their members. There is considerable evidence emerging from academic studies to indicate that countries which follow the broader concept of flexible working practices are economically more successful than those which stick to the narrower Thatcherite idea of flexible labour markets.

Demand-side and supply-side linkages

An issue that is not being adequately addressed is the link between demand and supply side policies. No one set of policies holds the key to economic success. Improvements on the supply side, however necessary and welcome, could amount to little if there is no demand for the goods and services supplied, however efficiently. Current fixations with the interest rate have consequences not only for demand, but also for the supply side, through effects on trade and investment. Through its influence on the exchange rate, the interest rate has a clear connection with competitiveness. If it is true, as some observers claim, that the pound has been at times overvalued, perhaps to the extent of 10-25%, then UK traders have been working with a considerable handicap.

For some time the so-called 'weakness' of the euro worsened the problem of the 'strength' of the pound. However during 2008 the euro began to rise slightly against the pound, alleviating the problem for UK manufacturers a little (but making holidays more expensive for UK tourists in the eurozone). During 2008-9, the euro and the pound came close to parity, and some commentators believed that this radically undermined arguments against Britain finally joining the euro.

Also, during 2008-9 there was a substantial fall in the value of the dollar, so that the exchange rate came very close to $2 = £1 for the first time in many decades. This made UK exports appear substantially more expensive when sold in the USA, but created a boom in the number of Britons making shopping expeditions from the UK to places like Boston and New York. On the other hand, American tourists were discouraged from holidaying in the UK due to the reduced purchasing power of the dollar over here. The 'good' news, however, was that since both oil and goods from China tend to be denominated in dollars when traded internationally, there were downward influences on prices in the UK.

Chapter 6

Why are exchange rates important?

How does trade affect exchange rates?

There is no such thing as 'the' exchange rate of the pound. The pound has as many exchange rates as there are other currencies in the world. However, if the pound moves in one direction against the currency of a major trading partner, it is likely (but not necessarily so) that it will move similarly against other major currencies also.

Suppose a British TV executive wishes to purchase some episodes of 'Family Guy' from the production company in the United States. Since pounds cannot be spent in California or Florida, those episodes have to be paid for in dollars. At some stage in the importing process, then, pounds have to be exchanged for dollars. We can visualise this as an increase in the supply of pounds on the international currency markets, and an increase in the demand for dollars.

Figure 6.1: A fall in the £ rate to the $

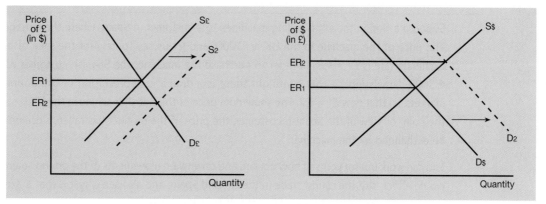

Figure 6.1 shows how imports from the USA into the UK at one and the same time increase the exchange rate of the dollar against the pound, and reduce the exchange rate of the pound against the dollar, assuming that there is a **freely floating** exchange rate (see Chapter 7 for a discussion of this term).

Now suppose that the BBC sells episodes of 'Gavin and Stacey' to a United States network. These will have to be paid for in pounds by the American TV company. On the foreign exchange markets we see an increase in the supply of dollars, and an increase in the demand for pounds, increasing the value of the pound against the dollar, and conversely reducing the value of the dollar against the pound. This is illustrated in Figure 6.2.

Figure 6.2: A rise in the £ rate to the $

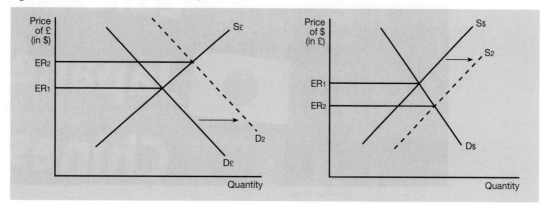

Apart from the volume of trade, other influences on the exchange rate of sterling include interest rates, inflation rates and relative prices, speculation and government action. All of these factors affect the demand and supply conditions of pounds and other currencies, as in the following examples.

- A rise in interest rates encourages people and organisations in other currencies to deposit money in UK financial institutions.

- If inflation is higher in the UK than in other countries, UK exports become less attractive over time in terms of price. The **purchasing power parity theory of exchange rates** suggests that if goods that are widely traded cost more in country A than in country B demand will shift away from A's products towards B's, thus reducing the exchange rate of the currency of A against the currency of B.

- It is estimated that more than 90% of trade in currencies is not to finance trade at all, but used instead to gamble on future exchange rate movements (see the 'confidence problem' below).

- Government policy can influence exchange rates either indirectly, by providing a sound business environment which encourages confidence in a currency, or directly by intervening in the markets to buy or sell currencies.

How do exchange rates affect trade?

Suppose a firm in the UK is selling machines to a customer in Spain, where the currency is the euro (€). The price of the machine in the UK is £1000, and let us say (purely for the sake of argument) that the exchange rate is £1 = €3. In order to purchase the machine, the Spanish customer will need to provide €3000. Now suppose that overnight there is a dramatic depreciation of the pound on international markets, so that now £1 = €2. The showroom price of the British machine in the UK is still £1000, but from the point of view of the Spanish customer, the price of the product has fallen, since only €2000 needs to be exchanged for the machine.

You can work out for yourself how upward and downward movements of the pound against other currencies would affect, say, the tourist trade in the UK and Spain; and also see why it is that a 'strong' pound (rising against other currencies) makes life difficult for UK exporters.

How do exchange rates affect trade?

The Marshall-Lerner condition

Exchange rate fluctuations in effect change *prices*. Consumer response to price changes is known as **price elasticity of demand**. Would a depreciation of the pound be helpful in reducing a balance of payments deficit? It depends on how UK consumers of imported goods and foreign importers of UK goods respond to respectively higher and lower prices. If the former respond by a larger percentage change in demand than and the latter, then overall changes in total revenue will improve the balance of payments.

The Marshall-Lerner condition suggests that depreciation will improve a balance of payments deficit if the price elasticity of demand for exports plus the price elasticity of demand for imports (both defined as a positive number) added together come to more than one (in other words, total demand for imports and exports is elastic).

Use a simple numerical example to illustrate this for yourself. Suppose that before depreciation exporters were selling 10 units at 10p each (total revenue 100p) and importers were buying 10 units at 12p each (total revenue 120p, and a deficit of 20p). Calculate what happens to the deficit if the elasticity of exports is 1 and the elasticity of imports is 0.5 (total elasticity greater than one); and if the elasticity of exports is is 0.6 and the elasticity of imports is 0.2 (total elasticity less than 1). Remember that price elasticity of demand = percentage change in quantity demanded divided by percentage change in price, and that total revenue is calculated by multiplying price times quantity.

The J-curve effect

Related to the Marshall-Lerner condition is the so-called **J-curve effect**. This idea suggests that in some countries, currency depreciation will worsen a country's balance of payments deficit before it starts to improve. This is because many countries, of which the UK is a prime example, need to import raw materials and components before they can sell exports.

Figure 6.3: The J-curve effect

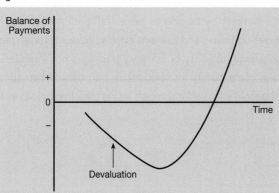

In other words, the demand for imports is inelastic in the short run, but the demand for exports is more elastic. Depreciation makes imports dearer, but imported products are needed to be turned into items to satisfy the increased demand for exports, hence the shape of the J-curve. This idea also helps explain why depreciation or a devaluation is often thought to be inflationary, at least in the short term, as it pushes up prices of commodities which continue to be purchased, and which feed into industrial costs.

Currency and exchange rates

We have already argued that international trade does not take place between 'nations' but between individuals and organisations within those nations. When Mexico imports machine parts from the USA, what actually happens is that a Mexican business has purchased machine parts from an American one. To pay for these imported goods, the Mexican firm has to obtain US dollars. This convention of paying for imports in the currency of the producing country means that most international trade is impossible without some system of currency exchange rates. There are exceptions: some trade is done in barter, and some in dominant 'hard' currencies that are more acceptable than local weak ones. Oil is usually denominated in US dollars throughout the world, although the European Central Bank is attempting to increase the use of the euro internationally for basic commodities that are traded around the globe.

The international exchange rate system has three general problems associated with it: the liquidity problem, the adjustment problem, and the confidence problem.

The liquidity problem

For international trade to take place, there must be international liquidity to pay for that trade. Unfortunately, there is no such thing as a world currency. Because of its special qualities as a precious metal, gold is perhaps the nearest thing that we have to a generally acceptable international medium of exchange, though its importance has declined in the last twenty years and reserves to back currencies have been allowed to run down, and governments have been selling off their gold reserves. As a substitute for gold, traditionally 'hard' currencies (normally with relatively stable exchange rates) have been used. These include the dollar, yen, the old German Deutschmark, and now the euro.

The adjustment problem

Fixed exchange systems, where exchange rates remain unchanged for long periods, provide a good climate for those involved in international trade. Export revenues and import bills can be predicted. Even more certainty could come from a global currency, but with major trading nations such as Britain unable to come to terms with a single currency even for Europe, a global currency at the present time looks like a mere fantasy.

In 1973 the Bretton Woods system of fixed exchange rates was abandoned in favour of floating exchange rates. Arguments surrounding fixed and floating regimes are discussed in Chapter 7.

The confidence problem

It is often suggested that exchange rate volatility increases uncertainty and reduces business confidence. It makes it more difficult for firms to estimate costs and revenues in advance, and thus harms world trade. It also leads to problems from speculators who, in effect, gamble on future movements of currencies. Economists generally agree that a certain amount of speculation is a positive thing, since it ensures that there is always someone willing to buy a currency, at whatever price it reaches, however high or low; speculators can help to stabilise markets by buying as prices fall and selling as prices rise. However, excessive speculation does the exact opposite, and worsens existing trends through bandwagon effects. It is a worrying fact that the overwhelming majority of currency trading is not intended to finance trade in the real world economy, but takes place purely for speculative purposes. When speculators undermine confidence in a currency, it is real people who suffer through losing their livelihoods as the productive base of an economy is eroded.

Chapter 7

Should Britain join the 'euro'?

Fixed and floating exchange rates

Back in the 1960s, when there was an international system of fixed exchange rates, the Labour government faced a crisis when it devalued the pound. Today, devaluations and revaluations take place every day with little comment. Under the old 'Bretton Woods' system of fixed exchange rates, currencies were aligned to each other by international agreement, and were allowed to change by only very small amounts in response to supply and demand only within rigid bands. If there was pressure on a country's exchange rates governments, through their central banks, had to use changes in interest rates, together with the buying and selling of gold and currency reserves, to maintain a fixed price.

Floating exchange rates are allowed to find their own level on world markets, determined by international supply and demand, without government intervention. A currency with a fixed exchange rate is pegged to another currency or 'basket' of currencies at a pre-determined rate, and either kept exactly to that rate or only allowed to fluctuate within agreed bands. If the currency appears to be moving out of its bands, then the monetary authorities take action, for example by selling the currency and reducing interest rates (to lower the exchange rate) or buying the currency (using foreign currency reserves) and raising the interest rate in order to raise the exchange rate.

Floating exchange rates are considered to have several advantages and disadvantages. Two advantages of floating exchange rates are very clear.

1. **Automatic adjustment.** Floating rates automatically adjust balance of payments equilibrium. If a country is in deficit, its exchange rate will fall, making exports cheaper and imports dearer, and thus reducing the deficit. If a country is in surplus, its exchange rate will rise, making exports dearer and imports cheaper, and thus reducing the surplus.

2. **Greater policy choices.** Floating rates give freedom of choice in domestic policy. Because they are automatic, the government is free to pursue policies in the domestic economy independently of balance of payments considerations.

But there are also disadvantages of floating exchange rates which we can identify.

1. **Exchange rate uncertainty.** Traders are uncertain as to what exchange rate movements are likely to take place in the future. For example, a British holiday company needs to order hotel beds in Spain for its next summer season. It has to pay for these beds in euros, but does not know in advance the value of the euro against the pound.

2. **Greater speculative activity.** Because of this uncertainty, speculators are tempted to 'gamble' on future exchange rate movements.

3. **Currency instability and collapse.** Excessive speculation can cause currencies to collapse, especially when speculators panic. Even essentially sound currencies can be subjected to a 'self-fulfilling prophecy' when a rumour spreads that its price is going to fall, and panic selling actually precipitates a collapse.

It is claimed that fixed or managed exchange rates reduce these risks and impose discipline in economic management. However, problems arise when currencies are fixed at a rate which is unrealistically high or low. An exchange rate which is too low can cause inflation due to the high prices of imports; an exchange rate which is too high can cause recession through a slump in exports, ultimately causing unemployment.

The euro can be viewed as an attempt to achieve some of the advantages of both fixed and floating systems.

The Single European Currency (the euro) can be viewed as an attempt to achieve some of the advantages of both fixed and floating systems. European countries which are closely involved in trade with each other achieve the stability and predictability of fixed exchange rates; since the euro can float against other non-euro currencies, there is some flexibility and room for adjustment as well.

On 1 January 1999, eleven of the fifteen members of the EU locked their currencies into the euro, forming a currency bloc which is becoming known as 'Euroland'. The founding members of Euroland were Austria, Belgium, Finland, France, Germany, Ireland, Italy, Luxembourg, Netherlands, Portugal, and Spain. They were soon joined by Greece, so that when euro notes and coins began circulation on 1 January 2001, the UK was at that time one of only three EU countries (along with Denmark and Sweden) that remained outside this venture. On 1 January 2007 Slovenia became the thirteenth member of the eurozone, Malta and Cyprus on January 1, 2008, and Slovakia on January 1, 2009. At the time of writing Lithuania and Estonia are committed to joining in 2010 and 2011 respectively, making 18 members altogether.

Responsibility for monetary policy among euro members has been transferred to the **European Central Bank** (ECB) in Frankfurt, which consists of representatives of each of the central banks of the thirteen euro member states.

In order to qualify for membership of the euro, countries had to match several 'convergence criteria', which mainly affected interest rates and government borrowing. Although there were some accusations of 'fudging' the statistics, the achievement of the convergence criteria was quite remarkable: in 1989, for example, Spain's interest rates were above 15%; by 1999 they were below 4%. Shortly after the creation of the euro, the ECB brought Eurozone interest rates down below 3%, around two percentage points below UK levels at that time. It is ironic that Britain, if it so wished, would have qualified for euro membership on the basis of the convergence criteria. However, British politicians argued that the time was not right in the 'economic cycle'. In reality, it is more accurate to say that the time was not right in the *political* cycle, since the government had committed itself to a referendum, which it could not be sure of winning in the face of opposition from a generally Europhobic press.

What would be the effects of Britain joining the euro? Let us examine some arguments against, together with some counter-arguments.

Arguments about the UK joining the euro

1. **There would be a loss of sovereignty**

   However, this is a suspect argument because existing sovereignty is largely phoney. Nation states are too small by themselves to counteract the power of huge multinational corporations in globalised markets.

2. **There would be a loss of independent monetary policy, and a 'one size fits all' interest rate**

   However, the regions of Britain already have had an unhappy experience of a 'one size fits all' interest rate, with the Bank of England setting a rate which suits the overheated housing market in the south-east, but spelt disaster for manufacturers in the north and west. Eurozone interest rates have consistently been lower than British ones. Critics of the single Eurozone interest rate appear to have forgotten that for nearly thirty years, the EU has operated cohesion and structural funds. These are transfers of expenditure towards the less developed countries and regions of Europe. Such transfers take up nearly half the EU budget, and form the basis of a coherent fiscal and budgetary policy designed to counteract the less desirable effects of a single monetary policy.

3. **The euro is unworkable and the system will probably break up**

   However, this is unlikely, since there is more flexibility in the Single European Currency arrangements than there was in the rigid Exchange Rate Mechanism. Press comment in the UK during the early months of the euro in 1999 focussed on the so-called 'weakness' of the euro, when its exchange rate fell against the dollar and the pound. However, this movement was largely due to temporary sluggishness in the German economy. Also, it should be remembered that a 'strong' currency is not necessarily a good thing. While the anti-euro press could hardly hide their glee at the 'weak' euro, UK manufacturers and exporters found themselves forced into near recession by the 'strong' pound.

4. **The UK will be locked in with the pound at too high a rate**

   This is possibly the most serious potential problem, as politicians tend to regard exchange rates in a 'macho' way and regard currency depreciation as a personal defeat. However, many economists argued that the pound was at too high a rate for many years, causing serious recessionary pressures especially in manufacturing. In 2008, following the credit crunch and recession the pound and the euro came close to parity and in early 2010 the euro was trading at about 91p in terms of sterling.

5. **Unemployment will rise**

   The imposition of a single currency across Europe means a single interest rate. Critics say that in countries like France and Germany, this interest rate is likely to be too high to stimulate a sluggish economy, whereas in countries like Portugal and Spain, historically accustomed to even higher interest rates, consumers are likely to act like irresponsible children given access to a credit card by their parents. The policy response from the ECB would be to ratchet up the interest rate still further to counteract demand-pull inflation, and thus worsen the problems of the larger economies. However, from Britain's point of view, the counter-argument would be that the UK economy is more flexible, especially with regard to its labour market, than those of France and Germany, and therefore better able to adjust to anti-inflationary policy without sacrificing employment.

6. **Mobility of labour in Europe is too low and labour markets are inflexible**

   It is important to remember that the Single European Market is to do with more than the free trade in goods and services between member countries. It also allows free movement of capital, and crucially, free movement of labour. EU countries must make better progress in such areas as mutual recognition of qualifications, so that people who wish to work in other parts of Europe may do so. A particular problem in the UK is our comparative lack of modern language skills. Better performance by our

education system in this sphere is probably the single most significant thing that could be done to improve the mobility of labour, and so to ensure that those people who wish to move to where the jobs are can do as they wish.

7. Wage differences will cause problems

Even though interest rates will be the same across Europe, there will still be wage differences. This will lead to inequalities, and widen gaps in living standards. However, economic theory predicts that capital will be drawn to low cost areas, and so relatively low wages in, say north-east England or mid Wales should, in the long run, move closer to the European average, provided that action is taken to overcome other obstacles to the mobility of capital, such as poor industrial infrastructure or lack of good transport facilities in the peripheral regions.

8. There are costs of conversion

An argument which is often put up in favour of the euro is that of **transaction costs**. Changing currencies costs money. If, before 1 January 1999, you were to take £100 today and change it into pesetas, then change the pesetas into francs, and so on working through the EU's fifteen currencies, then you would probably have ended up with about £25, and lost £75 in commission to the banks and *bureaux de change*. The euro removes such transaction costs. It should be remembered, however that entering the euro presents initial costs, for example shopkeepers and banks will have to re-programme their tills and computers. All businesses will have to re-print their catalogues and price lists. They will need to be convinced that the long-run advantages will outweigh these short-term costs.

9. The single market is separate from the single currency

However, the idea of a single market is illogical without a single currency. Even more important than transactions costs are the considerations of the single market. The main purpose of the single market is to give economies of scale. When Europeans go on holiday to the United States of America, they notice that the prices of many goods and services appear very cheap when compared with prices at home. This is mainly due to two reasons. Firstly, the USA has vigorous pro-competition laws, and monopolistic practices are more robustly challenged by the authorities than they are in Europe. Secondly, when American producers put a good or service on the market, they have a continent-wide market of 200 million people available to them (even more when the North Atlantic Free Trade Area encompassing Canada and Mexico is considered). This gives tremendous economies of scale.

The fact that in the EU's so-called single market there were as many currencies as there were member states represented a barrier to economies of scale. Now that the EU has 27 member states, the complete removal of this barrier would create a market of over 400 million people, even larger than the USA. Firms would be able to increase the specialisation of plant, for example a firm producing cosmetics could make all its toothpaste in the UK, all its deodorants in Spain, all its perfume in France, for example, and then sell these products across the entire continent. This specialisation would bring down prices.

Another aspect of the single market is the idea of **price transparency**. With goods and services priced in euros, companies would no longer be able to hide behind an exchange rate smokescreen. Politicians have become increasingly vocal about what has been called 'rip-off' Britain with car manufacturers, for example, being accused of charging much higher prices in the UK than European consumers would tolerate. The euro could therefore provide a major boost to competition policy.

An entry into the euro cannot be made overnight. Forward planning will be necessary. Even if Britain had wished to join the first wave, then it would probably not have been a practical proposition, because of the lack of preparation. Not least, a programme of public education will be necessary, so that the public are prepared. A comparable exercise occurred during the preparation for decimalisation in the late 1960s, and there was a lot of concern then that the public were not totally prepared, that they lost track to some extent of the value of money after the changeover, and that this enabled producers and retailers to increase prices, giving a boost to inflationary pressures. This would be completely unacceptable in the case of euro conversion.

From the consumer's point of view, a perhaps overwhelming argument in support of the euro is its anti-inflationary bias. However, in their role of employees, these consumers will have to weigh the advantages of being in a low-cost, low inflation, and therefore low-price market, against the possible disadvantages of being in a low wage, high unemployment economy.

Short-term technical adjustments such as costs of conversion are less important than long-term considerations that focus on strategy and the single market. This author holds that the overwhelming argument in favour of Britain's membership of the euro is the boost it would give to long term planning. Freed from the uncertainty of exchange rate movements within the Eurozone, businesses would be able to plan ahead. In a country like Britain, which needs to significantly increase its long-term investment levels, this is a crucial consideration.

By staying out of the first waves of participants in the euro, the UK may already have given its businesses trading disadvantages. However, the question of participation is as much a political issue as an economic one, and so the government may merely have made a realistic assessment of the support that the euro could expect from the UK electorate at this stage.

Although this chapter has at least attempted to focus on the economic as opposed to the political or social, in the final analysis the question of whether we should abandon the pound and join the euro becomes a wider debate about the type of society in which we in the UK wish to live. There is a wider debate ultimately revolving around where we see ourselves in the future. Is it as passive recipients of an American economic and business culture, or as leading members of a confident and distinctive Europe?

In 2008-2009 British exports slumped during the world recession. Member countries of the euro which had continued to commit themselves to manufacturing (led by Germany and France) proved much more able to resist the effects of recession than those that, like the UK had relied heavily on an inflated housing and property market to finance consumer spending, notably Ireland and Spain, although Spain also weathered aspects of the recession better than most due to its more effective regulation of its banking sector. While different countries within the Eurozone had different experiences during the recession, the overall effect was that the euro strengthened against the pound, so that the two currencies came quite close to parity.

On the face of it, this would have been an ideal time for the UK government to re-launch its official policy of joining the euro 'when the time is right'. Indeed, the government of Iceland, which like the UK had been relying heavily on financial services as a growing economic sector (and which does not even belong to the EU) began to seriously consider applying to adopt the euro as its national currency. Iceland felt that membership of a powerful currency bloc would help protect its economy from unpredictable changes in the global economy. However, in the UK there was not even a whisper of this possibility in official circles. This is probably a reflection of a political fact rather than the economics of the situation in which the UK found itself. Much of the tabloid press in the UK takes an anti-European stance, and leading politicians appear to believe that they must follow a tabloid agenda when they 'spin' their policies in the daily news. The result is that former Conservative Chancellor, Kenneth Clarke, an EU enthusiast, has said, it is impossible in the current climate to have a rational debate about Britain's membership of the euro, and it remains a long-term project rather than an immediate possibility.

Chapter 8

Globalisation: what is it?

Europe since the mid 1980s: the global context

Not so very long ago, in 1974, Anthony Sampson was able to publish an in-depth investigation into the world-wide affairs of an American multinational conglomerate (*The Inside History of ITT*) without once using the word 'globalisation'. Today, this word is heard on a daily basis, but it rarely benefits from a definition or a critical discussion of the phenomenon it describes.

Globalisation is what is known as a contested concept. While some writers approach it empirically others are normative: empirical writers endeavour to report on the causes and effects of globalisation, while normative writers see globalisation as something good or bad, and seek to promote or condemn it accordingly. Alternatively they might argue that it is a myth, and that the national state still matters.

An example of a normative commentator who strongly supports globalisation is the American writer Thomas Friedman, who describes the spread of capitalist values and networks around the globe as being accompanied by a 'golden straitjacket'. If a country wants to prosper through the use of information and communications technology, access to world markets, and inward investment, he claims, then it has to accept the rules of the global club which are low corporate and personal taxation, privatisation, deregulation, and free movement of capital. Ulrich Beck, on the other hand, takes a sceptical view. He describes globalisation as a 'thought virus' which has stricken political parties and the news media, and as a kind of 'economic new ageism', a revivalist movement whose apostles and prophets, instead of handing out leaflets at underground stations, preach the salvation of the world in the spirit of the marketplace. Similarly, John Gray of Cambridge University has described globalisation as a 'myth' and Paul Hirst of University College London has argued that the national still matters.

Is globalisation, then, a set of specifically new processes in the real world, or is it 'hype'? It is quite possibly both of these things at the same time. It is possible that globalisation reflects a 'win', or a series of 'wins'. We can identify lots of winning contests such as the north over the south, America over the Soviet Union, the west over the east, neo-liberalism over socialism, capital over labour, management over unions, laissez faire over Keynesian intervention, markets over governments, individualism over communal solidarity, 'stand-on-your-own-feet' over the welfare state, 'trickle-down' theory over income re-distribution. If such 'wins' have in effect been claimed by the enthusiasts of globalisation, then it is possible that a useful piece of terminology is missing from the current debate: it would be helpful to distinguish between globalisation and **globalism**. Globalisation merely describes a process that may or may not be going on. Globalism, like most other 'isms', describes a belief that this is the best way of doing things. If this distinction were more widely made and discussed, then it would then be easier to identify those empirical developments that may or may not be eroding the influence of nation states (these can be described as **globalisation**). This distinction would separate globalisation from the beliefs and actions of people and institutions who regard the globalising of economic life as a project, and who seek to impose a particular world view of the way in which governments and citizens should seek to manage matters such as free trade, privatisation, the provision of public services, and policies for the environment (this can be described as **globalism**). It can be argued that globalism has caused governments to believe that they must convince financial markets of their strength of purpose in implementing anti-inflation policy. This has reduced policy options. Fiscal adjustments became less and less available to governments that convinced themselves that headline reductions in tax rates were necessary for electoral success, while the deregulation of money markets led to an emphasis on the 'single golf club' of interest rate adjustments. The movement towards a Single European Currency reinforced policy convergence with the euro's growth and stability pact operating as a

European version of the globalist straitjacket. As we see in Chapter 17, however, the credit crunch and recession, has initiated in many quarters a major re-think about the mission of the globalists. At the same time, accelerating concerns about climate change, culminating in the Copenhagen Conference of December 2009, caused policy makers to reconsider some fundamental ideas about international income distribution and the sustainability of global economic growth.

Perceptions are important. Hype or not, if policy makers perceive something which is actually best described as **globalism**, but is widely described as **globalisation** to be a reality – whether that reality appears to be an opportunity or a threat – and then decide that policy responses are required, then those policy responses can have very real consequences in a wide range of important domains, including people's employment prospects and working conditions, their public services and their pensions entitlements. Have politicians swallowed the propaganda of the globalists, and allowed themselves to be convinced that they can no longer ask their voters to pay sufficient taxes to finance social needs such as public services, health systems, education, housing and pensions? It is a worrying thought that the leading evangelists of globalism are often highly-paid executives and directors of multinational companies who have a vested interest in the privatisation of public services. These people can afford to isolate themselves from poor quality public provision by paying privately for their own health, education and retirement needs. Yet when it came to the credit crunch many of these free-market capitalists were very quick to appeal to the taxpayer for funding when banks which had become 'too big to fail' collapsed as a result of their incompetent management and leadership. To many observers, this exposed the globalist project as a sham, designed to privatise the profits of international financial deals, while nationalising the losses. From this point of view, globalisation looks less like a world-wide natural phenomenon, but more like special pleading from a privileged section of society who stand to reap its benefits while imposing the costs on others.

But exactly what is globalisation? As happens so often in the modern media, we have been discussing this idea without attempting to say exactly what it is.

A definition

Internationalisation of trade has of course been taking place for centuries but economists argue that globalisation is not quite the same thing and has only been taking place for decades, coinciding with new communication technologies and the liberalisation of money and capital markets. A simple and memorable definition of 'globalisation', was promoted in 1996 by Peter Jay, then the BBC's Economics Correspondent. It was based on an earlier description of how globalisation works in practice suggested by the monetarist economist Milton Friedman, and is as follows:

> *"The ability to produce any good (or service) anywhere in the world, using raw materials, components, capital and technology from anywhere, sell the resulting output anywhere, and place the profits anywhere."*

Global free trade is clearly beneficial to the managers and shareholders of the multinationals, who would like nothing better than to receive profits generated from the economies of scale that would be created if everyone in the world were to drive the same motor car, eat the same hamburger, or wear the same baseball cap. Some observers believe that globalisation has automatic benefits for the majority of the world's population. Such observers tend to believe in a **trickle-down theory** of economic distribution. They believe that although globalisation might lead to a more unequal share-out of the world production cake, it will result in a bigger overall cake and thus benefit poorer sections of world society as well as the better off. Other observers believe that growth of the cake will be insufficient to benefit everyone, and that the 'haves' will take progressively bigger slices than the 'have-nots'.

The World Bank (IBRD) tends to favour the trickle-down view. It believes that there is a positive correlation between freeing markets and trade and the eradication of poverty in the long term. It asserts that there is no evidence that free trade pushes down wages for unskilled workers and that world growth is the most

promising way to reduce poverty in the LDCs (Less Developed Countries). Economists involved with the United Nations Development Programme (UNDP), on the other hand, are not so sanguine about the benefits of free trade. The view from the UN is that increased global competition does not automatically bring faster growth and development. Given this view the UNDP holds that in almost all LDCs that have undertaken trade liberalisation unemployment has increased and unskilled wages have fallen. Thus in their view growth in the world economy in the foreseeable future will be too slow to significantly reduce poverty. One way of viewing 'global development' is in terms of 'de-pauperisation', and countries need to act in concert in order to strive for this.

If global free trade is such a good thing, why are so many countries grouping themselves into regional trading blocs? In Europe, in particular, this trend is not just **regionalisation**; to many people it is also based on **regionalism** – a belief that this is a worthwhile action in its own right. A substantial minority of economists are arguing that protectionism is not always a bad thing, and that protective barriers might surround some things that actually are worth protecting, such as a distinctive culture, or a region which depends on a particular industry for its way of life. Regionalisation occurs partly in response to the success of the European Union, partly as a reaction to the challenge to the nation-state presented by globalisation. Is the trend contrary to global free trade? If North and South America, Africa, and the Asia/Pacific form regional trading groups, then LDCs might find themselves seriously disadvantaged. The arguments advanced against the protectionism of the EU would apply equally to these other blocs. Essentially, the arguments are two-fold: firstly, the export of EU surpluses to LDCs constitutes the 'dumping' of foodstuffs at low prices; secondly, trade barriers deny the LDCs access to markets within the EU.

The World Bank and other influential commentators have become increasingly critical of the Common Agricultural Policy of the EU and its other equivalents around the world, including the farm support programmes of the US government. These critics estimate that taxpayers and consumers in OECD countries are paying hundreds of billions of pounds each year in farm support and protection. Paradoxically, less than half of this money actually benefits producers as mostly it results in the long run in higher land prices or rents. Artificially high prices raise output inefficiently, and they also discriminate against imports. Less developed countries are refused access to western markets for their agricultural products, and this is because their products are too cheap! This idea would cause free-market economists like Smith and Ricardo to spin in their graves, and since LDCs often rely on agriculture for 30-40% of GDP this is harming economic development around the world.

Trade creation and trade diversion

Do regional trading blocs increase or decrease world economic welfare? Do they accelerate or decelerate the move towards global free trade? It all depends on the difference between **trade creation** (the ability of freer trading arrangements to generate new output) and **trade diversion** (the tendency for trading blocs to redistribute existing output to different trading partners rather than to increase the total amount of output). A trade bloc improves global welfare only if it creates more trade than it diverts. If neighbouring countries already trade significantly with each other, the removal of tariffs will probably increase the gains from specialisation and trade, unless their new common tariff wall creates a barrier to more efficiently-produced imports from non bloc countries. However, neighbouring countries do not necessarily have big trade flows with each other: African countries, for instance export 95% of their goods to countries outside Africa.

Trading blocs between MDCs (More Developed Countries) are likely to be successful. Academic studies usually conclude that EU GDP is several percentage points higher than it would have been without the existence of the organisation. But this implies a net gain in trade creation over trade diversion, and the trade diversion may well have been at the expense of LDCs which were part of the former trading and political empires of countries like France and Britain.

African countries export 95% of their goods to countries outside Africa.

Trading blocs between LDCs are unlikely to yield large welfare gains. However, a bloc including LDCs and large MDCs (such as a link between North and South America) could have benefits, since it would guarantee access to a large market and thus encourage economies of scale. The low cost labour of the LDC would find itself in the same regional trading bloc as the low cost capital of the MDC. Here the relationship between the USA and Mexico within NAFTA since January 1994 is of particular interest. American exports to Mexico have increased substantially, although Mexico achieved a trade surplus with the USA. American officials claim NAFTA as an important factor moving Mexico towards prosperity, and argue that this justifies the opening of trade negotiations with Chile and other Latin American and Asian countries. Trade creation would seem to have taken place. However whether unemployed US blue-collar workers whose jobs have been exported to the low wage area of Mexico would be convinced by 'welfare gain' arguments is a moot point.

The EU has expanded to include central and eastern European countries; and it is possible that other Latin American countries could join NAFTA. Such expansion could actually be counterproductive if fears of being shut out of these two groups cause Asian countries to set up an FTA of their own. In South East Asia, the ASEAN group is already in the process of substantially reducing tariffs on nearly all intra-ASEAN trade, and removing most non-tariff barriers to imports. Much depends on the future of the World Trade Organisation; if it fails, members might fall back on FTAs which then could turn out to be anything but a stepping stone towards global free trade.

As Peter Jay's definition suggests, multinational companies can increasingly produce goods anywhere in the world, sell their output anywhere, using resources and technology from anywhere, and place the resulting profits anywhere. In order to promote globalisation, 'free trade' agreements have been entered into and any country wishing to share in the alleged benefits of globalisation must disavow 'protectionism'.

Globalisation has its less benign side as it enables firms to produce in low-wage countries where environmental legislation is weak, then sell this output in high income countries where markets are strong, and report its accounts in low-tax countries. The outcome is that they achieve maximum profitability with minimum social responsibility or accountability. One of the most famous sportswear companies, for example, uses American basketball stars to endorse its products, but employs no manufacturing staff in

the USA. This is because its training shoes are made in the Third World by people employed for a few pence per hour before being sold at as high a price as the market will bear in the affluent west!

UK policy-makers appear to have wholeheartedly accepted the idea of globalisation, and like other countries operating in the global economy, the UK is constrained by what has been called the 'golden straitjacket'. If a country wants to have access to global communications, information technology, world markets and inward investment, then it has to accept the rules of 'club' membership mentioned earlier – low taxes, privatisation, deregulation, and free movement of capital.

It is argued in the next chapter that regional blocs are a countervailing power which governments can use to protect their positions against multinational corporations whose annual revenues are larger than the gross domestic product of many nation-states, and that they can be beneficial – particularly to their less advantaged citizens – if they help to ameliorate the harsher effects of globalisation. If, for instance, right-wing governments in Europe were to assert their nationalism and oppose Europe-wide social legislation, then multinationals might be given free reign to drive down wages, worsen working conditions, and pollute the environment.

As is argued in Chapter 11, a substantial minority of economists are arguing that protectionism is not always a bad thing, and that protective barriers might actually surround some things that are worth protecting, such as a distinctive culture, or a region which depends on a particular industry for its way of life.

Globalised labour

While capital has become globalised, and there is free movement of wealth, wealthy persons, and the managerial class across the globe, the free movement of labour has not kept pace. While business corporations have lost no time in going global, labour organisations have been slow off the mark, although some trade unions are at last beginning to try to catch up, by forming alliances with their counterparts in other countries. From the union point of view, it makes sense if, in negotiating with an employer based in, say, Detroit, but with plants in, say, Swansea, Lyons and Valencia, the union has, through its alliances, members belonging to branches in each of those cities. This would help redress the balance of power between capital and labour and reduce the chances of the employer 'playing off' one country's workforce against another.

Now that the EU has expanded to 27 member countries, there is a single market covering most of the continent of Europe. If, as many people hope, the Ukraine and Turkey eventually join, then the EU will even spill out of geographical Europe and into Asia. The single market allows free movement of goods and services, free movement of capital, and free movement of labour. This last feature is both new and old, but even now so-called globalisation stops far short of allowing labour markets to go truly global. Indeed, certain sections of our media, and some of our politicians, appear haunted, agitated and obsessed by the idea of migrant workers 'flooding' from one country to another, and 'swamping' so called 'indigenous' populations. Yet there are very few families in Britain (or anywhere else) who do not have 'asylum seekers', 'refugees' or 'economic migrants' within two or three generations of their immediate family tree. The work of the geneticist Professor Sykes would suggest that most readers of this book could trace their ancestry through their DNA to one of seven women who were alive around 30,000 years ago; and anthropologists such as the Doctors Leakey, have shown that originally we all come from ancient ancestors in East Africa. It does not matter who we think we are, if we trace our family tree back far enough (and in most cases not very far), we inevitably find that we all come from somewhere else, each and every one of us, and in this sense the idea of an 'indigenous' population is meaningless. These are sobering thoughts for racists and bigots everywhere.

There is, therefore, a crucial element missing from current debate about globalisation or globalism. Before the First World War it was possible to travel across the continent without a passport. When Britain had 'open' borders she was also an undisputed industrial, naval and military power. Was this coincidence of free movement of labour and economic success 'mere' correlation or was there some cause and effect? Either way, these facts appear now to be largely ignored, or conveniently forgotten, often by the very politicians who regularly lecture us about the 'inevitability' of globalisation as a fact of life. Perhaps we should question far more rigorously those in authority, and their collaborators in the less responsible sections of the media, who promote the free movement of goods, services and capital as some kind of natural phenomenon, but who seek at the same time to stir up fear and hatred of the free movement of people.

Chapter 9

Globalisation: who needs it?

Globalisation, regionalisation and European integration

When Britain joined the European Economic Community (later to become the European Union) in 1973, economists and political scientists studying European integration focused their attention on what was essentially a set of international organisations that had been created by powerful national leaders such as President de Gaulle of France and Chancellor Adeneuer of Germany, and put together by high-profile international actors such as Jean Monnet and Paul-Henri Spaak who had designed new institutions on a grand scale.

Today, students of European integration are more likely to believe themselves to be focusing on a unique type of domestic economic and political system, which far from being a strongly federal 'United States of Europe' is a complex institution with multi-levelled structures. There are now more actors deemed worthy of serious academic attention: not only the international power-brokers but also political and civic actors at sub-national levels. Whether we regard ourselves as economists, or political scientists, or political economists, we have moved from the time when the EU was seen as purely a trading area, or a third-force power bloc placed between the USA and Soviet Union in the Cold War – an international organisation and little else – towards a position where many of its aspects are seen as belonging to a kind of domestic economy and policy. Many observers regard the regional level as the location of much of the interesting and even exciting action in contemporary Europe. Regionalism is developing at two levels, with supra-national regionalism (closer integration of nations located in the European region of the globe) moving in step with sub-national regionalism (growing support for devolution to sub-national democracies such as the Scottish Parliament and Welsh Assembly) with important economic development functions. At this sub-national regional level, there are at least four further important differences between the economic and political atmosphere of the early 21st Century when compared with the 1970s.

Firstly, there is the impact of globalisation. The geography of economic unevenness has become more complex. All regions now have pockets of unemployment and disadvantage. The 'prosperous' South East contains London boroughs some of whose wards are among the most disadvantaged in the UK. Wales, generally regarded on most indicators as a less advantaged region, contains council wards in, for example, Cardiff and the Vale of Glamorgan where income per head is on a par with European averages. Across the UK there is still a real north/south divide, but a simple set of south/north transfers is no longer regarded as a sufficient response. One reason for this is that in a context of globalisation, companies are no longer organised on a national basis. Firms no longer choose between regions within one nation-state as they are free to locate virtually anywhere in the world.

Secondly, in many cases regional actors no longer appear to need to feel obliged to react to globalisation by lying down in front of a road-roller that obliterates local culture. Far from being seen as a barrier to economic development, local culture and identity is increasingly being seen as a resource that can be utilised in a global context to stimulate development. Hence, 'laptops und lederhosen', as they say in Germany, as their version of the now well-known slogan 'think global, act local'. A possible reason why regions like Catalonia and cities like Barcelona are so widely regarded as 'role models' is because it is believed that Catalonia has reacted successfully to the opportunities and/or threats that globalisation appears to create.

The third difference is that regionalism is no longer seen in purely local terms. For example, the issues occupying the minds of Welsh political and business elites in the unsuccessful 1979 Welsh devolution referendum were different from those arising in the (just) successful 1997 campaign. From being a purely Welsh or British issue in 1979, devolution in 1997 was re-positioned as part of a Europe-wide phenomenon. Wales was re-cast as something called a 'European region', and use was made of references to 'role models' such as Catalonia and Ireland.

Fourthly, and this follows from the previous point, there is the growing phenomenon known as 'paradiplomacy', which sees regions attempting to exert influence as actors in their own right on the international scene, not only through representation in the corridors of power where interests need to be defended and cases for investment funds need to be made, but also in a range of inter-regional forums with a wide variety of aims. This phenomenon enables contact to be made between regional institutions with wide variations in terms of power and responsibility (often these institutions have actually been formally excluded from international relations in the traditional sense), allows regional governments to conduct a 'foreign policy' of sorts, and, crucially allows regions to learn from each other and to acquire a wish to extend their responsibilities.

Paradiplomacy can also be viewed as a political activity that underpins an economic strategy based on 'export-led growth'. Role model regions such as Catalonia are therefore anything but inward-looking. To the annoyance of the Madrid government, Catalonia has set up trade delegations in foreign capitals which look to all intents and purposes like embassies. Dynamic cities such as Barcelona are keen to promote themselves as globalised sorts of places with a distinctive life and culture of their own but with an outward view of the world.

Europe since the mid 1980s: the relaunch of integrative institutions

The mid-1980s can be regarded as a watershed period for several reasons. In macroeconomic terms, it confirms the fundamental shift of the 1970s from Keynesian aggregate-economy manipulation led by the state, to a new economic orthodoxy aimed at managing the remainder available for state intervention after the privatisations promoted by the Thatcher-Reagan axis. These reforms were reinforced by international de-regulation and the globalisation of product and financial markets. In British politics, what might be called an economic 'de-centralisation' of previously centralised, nationalised enterprises took place. Privatisation, which encompassed the sale of state assets, de-regulation, franchising and market testing, was 'de-centralising' in the sense that these changes were claimed to move public services further from the centralised bureaucracy and closer to the 'consumer'. This policy was anomalously accompanied by a concerted centralisation of many political processes to the organs of the nation-state, for example with an attack on local government autonomy in general and local control over certain services such as education in particular. This is further discussed in Chapter 15.

At the European level, Conservative Prime Minister Margaret Thatcher once famously defined her Euro-scepticism in terms of her economic and political world-view when she declared that she had not set about rolling back the frontiers of the state at national level only to see them re-imposed at the European Level. From this perspective, the EU is seen as an insidious superstate, thwarting the attempts of free-marketeers to persuade citizens to accept the facts of modern global life.

Another way of looking at the EU and its members is to recognise that modern nation states are quite 'fluid', reacting to changes from three directions. Firstly those arriving *from above* due to globalisation and Europeanisation. A second source of changes are those *from within* due to deregulation, privatisation, and new economic management. A third source of changes are those *from below* due to the influence of local authorities and regional assemblies.

Anthony Giddens of the London School of Economics has stated that while the EU began as a reaction to 'bi-polarism' (in the days of the Cold War when the world was dominated by two superpowers), today it is best understood as a reaction to globalisation. Globalisation is seen by many people as meaning almost the same thing as 'Americanisation'.

The training shoe is often given as an example of 'globalisation'.

If you ask the person in the street (or the student in the classroom) for an example of 'globalisation' in practice, they will almost invariably mention the influence of an American multinational enterprise, such as McDonald's or Microsoft. They will mention an example of the domination of world popular culture, such as the training shoe, the baseball cap, the TV comedy programme with its canned laughter and huge teams of highly-paid scriptwriters, or the violent and aggressively marketed Hollywood blockbuster, where explosions only harm villains, and where heroes speak the globalised language of English, but always with American accents.

Nations that by themselves are too small to stand up to the power of huge multinational companies are voluntarily pooling their sovereignty in order to counterbalance some of the undesirable results of globalisation. Contrary to the views of the Thatcherites and Britain's Eurosceptic press, the EU is neither simply an intergovernmental organisation nor a federal super-state. Instead it is a set of multi-levelled policy-making institutions reflecting a situation in which policy-making is not reserved for an exclusive set of actors, but is diverse with the EU encouraging the wide use of partnerships and networks of local actors. With this diversity comes a broad idea of development, to encompass not only narrow economic issues, but also quality of life, language, cultural activities, and political participation. Local cultures are less likely to be seen as obstacles to development in this new scheme of things. Instead they are seen as a resource which can help to create the networks, associations and collaborations necessary for development. Rather than accept the simplistic view of 'rolling back' the state, the state is being reinvented in an 'enabling' role, as Nineteenth Century institutions are redesigned for the Twenty-first Century.

The changes *from within* the European institutions occurring since 1979 came firstly from enlargement, with the accession of countries like Spain, Portugal, Denmark and Finland, so that membership rose to fifteen countries. Secondly, they came from the move towards a single market, which had its origins in the Cecchini report of the 1980s. This report identified the main impediments, such as different national practices, testing standards, and bureaucratic obstructions that stood in the way of free movement of goods, services, persons and capital within the European Community (EC). Based on a survey of some 11000 business people, it calculated that these impediments cost some 5% of GDP of the EC, and that their removal could give non-inflationary growth of 7% in the medium term while creating 5 million jobs. In essence, the argument was that consumers in Europe could benefit from US-style continent-wide economies of scale and advantages of specialisation. Thirdly, there were economic changes forced by the 'convergence criteria' needed for the adoption of a single currency (the 'euro'), which through their effects on government expenditure capabilities re-enforced the decline of welfare state economics and its replacement by a loosely defined 'Third Way'. Fourthly, there was a new stress on the regionalisation of European funding, which came to be a catalyst for changes in sub-national governance. Any countries wishing to benefit from EU funding for economic development had to be willing to allow the European Commission to work with regional partnerships. The strengthening of EU regional funds therefore went hand-in-hand with the strengthening of regional government throughout Europe.

These four trends taken together can be viewed as forming a major 're-launch' of the European institutions which began in the mid-1980s and can be largely (but not solely) attributed to Jacques Delors as President of the Commission. It was embodied in the Single European Act and Treaty of Maastricht, and followed in the 1990s by the single market and the single currency.

The Treaty of Lisbon, 2009

With a membership of 27, perhaps soon to grow into the early 30s, it became very difficult for the EU to govern itself efficiently. For example, the use of the 'veto' by any one state had to be reduced, otherwise the EU might become incapable of making any decision. At first, an attempt was made to write a 'constitution' for the EU, but in the face of opposition from Eurosceptics in several countries the terminology of 'constitution' was eventually dropped. In the autumn of 2009, the Treaty of Lisbon was finally ratified by all member states. Among its provisions was an agreement to create two key posts, a President of the European Council and a High Representative for Foreign Affairs and Security. Time will tell whether these developments will increase the standing of the EU as a group of countries on the global stage.

Anti-globalisation movements

British elite actors working in a number of contexts including the political, economic and cultural have often looked overseas for role models to guide policy development in the UK. British politicians often claim to have a 'special relationship' with the USA, and this idea has survived a number of events that logically should have killed it stone dead, from the Suez crisis of 1956 through the Falklands conflict of 1982 to the US withdrawal from Kyoto and the imposition of American tariffs on UK steel in the 1990s. In recent years, the resilient idea of a 'special relationship' has become inter-twined with an international 'role modelling' process whereby UK politicians seek policy inspiration from the USA. In the media, observers such as Will Hutton have commented on this tendency among British politicians. Hutton has argued that American power over Britain is not only corporate, military, financial and political but it is also intellectual and cultural. He argues that this has a tendency to push the norms and value-judgements in areas like social science and management steadily to the right. American values and policy are inserted into the British debate and cemented by the cultural impact of film, music and television. He argues that this happens despite the fact that British values are closer to Europe than those of American conservatism and that New Labour is under pressure to deliver improved public services and a more robust social safety-net. Hutton argues New Labour's own supporters distrust the borrowed American conservatism that informs many of its criminal justice and social policies. The march of the American conservative right is seen as having helped to undermine our conceptions of the proper relationship between the market and society. If Britain is to address its long-standing productivity problem or the weaknesses of its public services, it needs to be open to European examples and models rather than having its options locked in the American bear hug. Hutton concludes that in the same way that Britain should reappraise its relationship with American defence and security policy, so it must reappraise its relationship to American ideas of economic and social organisation. It is time the British recognised who they really are, not mere consumers in the fifty-first state of the USA, but full citizens of a country that is a leading actor in Europe.

In recent years economic summits and meetings of the WTO have attracted street demonstrations, and occasional disturbances. Around 1000 'anti-globalisation' and 'anti-capitalist' protesters were arrested during the Copenhagen climate change conference of December 2009. Naomi Klein's book protesting against the influence of the multinationals, *No Logo*, has become a best seller. In some quarters, great faith is placed in the idea of ethical consumerism, and it is possible to go to the supermarket armed with publications such as *The Good Shopping Guide*, whose publishers claim that 'your till receipt is as good as your vote'. The aim is to enable consumers to, for instance, buy a vacuum cleaner from a company that has no known links with the global arms industry, a washing powder from a company that does not damage the environment, or a pair of trainers that has not been made by a ten year old in a dangerous sweatshop. This book's first edition sold out its print run of 21,000. However, in his book *The Age of Consent*, George Monbiot, who is a leading member of a campaign called the 'Global Justice Movement' says that consumers trying to signal their ethical purchasing decisions through the price mechanism will find that the signal they are trying to send to producers gets lost in the 'general noise of the market'.

There are some famous examples of consumer boycotts that have had spectacular success. Barclays Bank was boycotted in the late 1960s, initially by students protesting at its international operations in the apartheid era, and eventually withdrew from South Africa. More recently Nestlé has been plagued by bad publicity about its supplies of powdered milk to African nursing mothers. Monsanto has withdrawn its GM products from European markets after major supermarkets refused to stock foods containing these ingredients as a direct result of consumer resistance. Yet campaigners claim that the processed food industry continues to assist in the killing of an estimated 5000 Britons a year through adding too much salt to its products, and children's television is full of persuasive advertising from toy and junk food producers, in spite of protests from consumer groups. Consumers can register their preferences by purchasing brands such as the 'Fairtrade' range available at Oxfam shops, cooperative stores, and increasingly in the large supermarkets, and these products promise to direct a larger proportion of revenues to the actual producers on the ground rather than the shareholders of multinationals. However, these products have to be sought out and there is a limited range.

It is also difficult for consumers to register a 'vote' against undesirable practices on the other side of the world by companies producing basic raw materials. George Monbiot gives the example of the market for copper. He claims that the indigenous people of West Papua in Indonesia have been badly treated by the owners of copper mines, but he points out that consumers do not buy copper directly. It is brought into the house by plumbers and electricians who have little choice as to which material to use, and passed down such a long supply chain that the final consumer has little chance of persuading the copper mine to behave more ethically.

Chapter 10

What are the choices in trade policy?

Trade and welfare

In this chapter we use the basic economic model of supply and demand to illustrate the gains from international trade. We then go on to consider basic choices that have to be made by policy makers in the light of these gains.

Figure 10.1: Consumer surplus

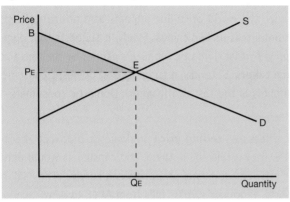

In what ways can economic welfare be increased by international trade? Figure 10.1 shows the market for a good in a closed economy; that is, an economy that does not take part in international trade. The good in question could be, for example, shoes; and the diagram shows the familiar supply and demand equilibrium. One way of attempting to measure economic welfare through trade is to consider the 'balance' between **consumer surplus** and **producer surplus**.

The demand curve can be regarded as indicating the maximum amount which consumers are willing to pay for the right to purchase a product. The difference between what the consumer is willing to pay and the actual price paid can be thought of as being 'free' satisfaction, or consumer surplus. If the equilibrium price is P_E, then every consumer to the left of Q_E receives consumer surplus and the total consumer surplus received is equal to area $P_E EB$. In economic theory, the rational consumer is said to desire maximum utility, and so an increase in consumer surplus can be taken to mean an increase in welfare.

Figure 10.2: Producer surplus

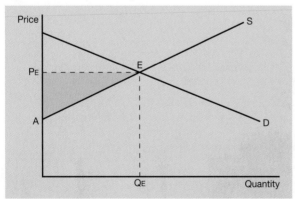

The supply curve can be taken to indicate the minimum return which is necessary to induce a producer to supply a product. Any surplus over and above this minimum return can be referred to as producer surplus. Producer surplus in Figure 10.2 is shown by area $AP_E E$. The theory of perfect competition makes much of the idea that although producers act in their own self interest in trying to maximise short-run profits, in the long run competition ensures that surplus profits disappear, and this is said to encourage an optimum use of resources. We can therefore conclude that a reduction in producer surplus is likely to correspond to an improved allocation of resources, and hence an increase in welfare.

Figure 10.3 shows the market for shoes after the closed economy has become an 'open' one, that is, after international trade starts to take place. The price is determined on the world market, where the world price P_W is established at the intersection of the world supply curve, S_W, and world demand, D_W. The world price is lower than the domestically determined price, reflecting in this case the greater efficiency of foreign producers over some but not all domestic producers, and the greater market size.

Figure 10.3: The impact of trade

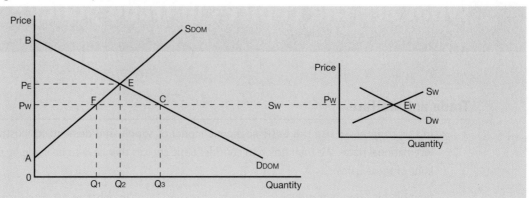

From the domestic point of view, the world price line appears as a horizontal supply curve, Pw-Sw. Assuming that this line is horizontal tells us two things. Firstly, it suggests that domestic production is small compared with world supply, so that domestic producers cannot by their own actions affect world price. They therefore act as **price takers**. Secondly, it suggests that domestic consumers could have their entire demand satisfied by suppliers in the rest of the world. Domestic consumers can buy an infinite quantity at the world price.

The world price Pw now acts in effect as a **ceiling price** on domestic producers, because if they tried to charge their equilibrium price PE, they would sell nothing, and consumers would only purchase cheaper imports. Hence only the most efficient domestic producers can survive. They sell quantity OQ1, and quantity Q1Q3 represents imports. Producer surplus falls from APEE to APwF, while consumer surplus increases from PEBE to PwBC. Consumer welfare has therefore increased, as a result of the *transfer of some producer surplus to consumer surplus*. It could also be argued that welfare has increased in other ways, since consumers are likely to find that through having imported shoes made available to them they have greater choice of materials, styles, and so on.

Suppose the domestic government were to restrict imports, for example with a tariff. In effect this would shift the horizontal world supply curve upwards (when viewed from the home country), and at least in the

Mumbai Harbour: India is now an example of an outward-orientated economy.

short term boost domestic production, increase consumer prices, and cause a reduction in efficiency. Hence the above analysis can be used to support the proposition that free trade is beneficial, and that trade restrictions lead to welfare losses.

Outward and inward orientation

Since international trade can increase welfare, economists generally argue that 'open' economies are the best. Countries which are open to world markets are described as **outward-orientated economics**. The 'Tiger Economies' of the far east have been widely quoted as examples, as has the recent development of the 'BRIC' economies (Brazil, Russia, India, China). Countries which protect their domestic markets from foreign competition and try to develop using their own resources are described as **inward-orientated economics**. Until comparatively recently, this was the policy of India, for example, and also of China in communist times.

Increasingly, since the 1990s, the appearance of **trade blocs** has allowed countries to have aspects of outward orientation in their relationships with fellow members inside a Free Trade Area, Customs Union or Common Market, while keeping some insulation against the extreme competition of world markets.

Outward orientation

One approach to trade is to concentrate on producing exports from the industrial sector. Adam Smith recognised as long ago as 1776 that specialisation, trade, exchange and hence the *Wealth of Nations* was limited by what he called the 'extent of the market'. Singapore (population: 3.0 million) and Hong Kong (6.2 million), both rich city-states, have relatively affluent domestic markets, but they are relatively small, so if they were to produce manufactured goods solely for the domestic market they would not benefit from mass production techniques. Instead, they manufacture far more than they can consume themselves, and export the surplus. In certain industries, such as the production of family cars, the state of technology and market conditions are such that there is a '**minimum efficient scale**', which means that in order to supply this market at all, a firm must produce millions of units to be profitable. Thus car manufacture becomes an **oligopolistic market structure**, i.e. it becomes dominated by fewer, larger firms. It also means that even quite populous countries like Korea (44.9 million in 1995) and Malaysia (21 million) have had to concentrate on export demand, because the home market is too small to produce sufficient economies of scale. This is done despite knowing that such a policy might worsen inequalities of income, since low cost labour is an important element in the international competitiveness of these countries. Outward orientation often means being open to foreign employers who are looking specifically for cheap labour markets with minimal regulations.

The newly-industrialised countries (NICs) have for many years exported items such as textiles and clothing to the more developed countries (MDCs), but they have more recently begun to develop markets for products such as steel, consumer goods, petrochemicals, electronics and cars. Often the finance, know-how, design and technology is imported from MDCs such as Japan, and combined with low cost labour which undercuts the wage costs of the MDCs by a margin with which producers in the MDCs can never hope to compete. The success of the Proton car in the UK is a case in point. It was designed in Japan and based on Japanese technology, but is built in Malaysia. It provides a five-door family saloon at a price range where there is virtually no competition, except from other products of the Tiger Economies. Kia, Daewoo, and the Proton actually penetrated the British car market during the worst part of the UK recession in the early 1990s.

A potential problem is that outward orientation puts countries at the mercy of changing world conditions. A world recession can cause export volumes to shrink, make the prices of exports unreliable, lead to protectionism on export markets, and cause difficulty for LDCs in repaying the loans that made industrialisation possible through purchasing fuel and machinery. In the MDCs, the real or imagined threat

from the NICs might also provoke allegations of **dumping**, or flooding their markets with goods at an 'unfairly' low price, and might prompt some sort of retaliation in the form of protectionism.

Inward orientation

Until the early 1990s countries like China and India, with large domestic markets, and with many natural resources of their own, were able to pursue a policy of exporting a great deal less than many other NICs, while meeting their own needs and replacing many imports with local products. In India, the domestic car market, for example, was not served by the multinationals like Ford and General Motors whose products are so well known in the MDCs. Instead of the Ford Escort, Indian streets are still thronged with the Hindustan Ambassador, a locally built version of the Morris Oxford, a well-known British car of the 1950s.

Smaller countries often experience serious difficulties with this approach. This is again because of the limited extent of the market. For example there might be too few customers to make up a mass market, or there might be many potential customers without the economic means to buy the products). Alternatively there may be a problem because of a lack of local resources, making the country dependent on imported raw materials which need to be paid for through exports.

An **import-substitution strategy** can also lead to stresses and strains when consumers demand access to goods and services which have become internationalised. In an age of world-wide telecommunications consumers everywhere are aware of the existence of such things as Coca-Cola and Nike sportswear and might not be willing to accept a locally-produced alternative. The advertising and branding activities of oligopolistic firms engaged in non-price competition are perceived throughout the world, and often give rise to standards for emulation. This is a belief on the part of consumers in LDCs that possession of branded goods from MDCs confers status. This helps explain why formula milk for babies and western cigarette brands can increase sales in LDCs although they actually arouse disapproval in their countries of origin. Keeping such brands out of a market through protectionism when they are associated with popular cultural icons such as the Michaels – Jordan and Jackson – can cause a government serious unpopularity.

There are powerful arguments based in economic theory for an open economy geared up towards trade. However, an advantage of the inward-orientation strategy is that it avoids problems associated with international payments and debt, a topic to which we shall return.

Chapter 11

Free trade 'good', protection 'bad'?

Types of protection

In the real world of international trade and globalisation the choice of whether to be outward or inward orientated is not the only choice to be made. Countries may have as many trade policies as they have trading partners, and no nation follows a policy of free trade in all goods and services. Since 1945 the average level of tariffs (import duties) has fallen substantially in trade between more developed countries (MDCs), from 40 per cent to less than five per cent, but protectionism has taken on many new forms despite the clear arguments for economic liberalism advocated by many economists.

Protectionism consists mainly of tariffs, quotas, voluntary export restraints, embargoes, subsidies, import licenses, local content agreements, health and safety legislation and international commodity agreements.

Arguments for and against protection

In all cases of trade restraints which are not negotiated, and which are therefore not voluntary, any argument in favour must be weighed against the possibility of retaliation. Retaliation can lead to 'trade wars' which can undermine the gains from trade for all participants. Why, then, is it sometimes argued that free trade should be suspended, and that protectionism can be justified?

1. Governments argue that it is necessary to protect certain **strategic industries** from competition. This is a political argument, rather than being solely economic, because the decision to define a certain industry as 'strategic' cannot be made on purely economic grounds. In a continent with a warlike history, it is not surprising that defence industries such as aircraft and shipbuilding have been heavily subsidised and protected from foreign competition. The fact that the EU countries protect their agricultural sector, for example, has more to do with the history and politics of Europe than it has to do with economic principles. In terms of economic efficiency, it is absurd that 60% of the budget of the EU should be devoted to an industry which employs 4% of the population, that the EU should spend taxpayers' money on maintaining surpluses of expensive farm products, and that farmers and fishermen should attack imports on the grounds that they are too cheap. If however, we trace the history of the EU to the immediate post-war years when there were shortages of food in the countries of western Europe, then we can understand how, at that time, food production was seen as a strategic industry, worthy of special treatment, even if that treatment discouraged imports and contravened Ricardian principles. Yet the result is that heavily subsidised, low quality tobacco enters the world market from Europe at prices that create the illusion of competitiveness, and keeps potentially more efficient but unsubsidised farmers in less developed countries (LDCs) out of trade.

   This type of protection is often used selectively and inconsistently. No doubt the coalminers of South Wales and the East Midlands would have welcomed the kind of protection that British farmers have traditionally received. As argued previously, a protective wall might surround things actually worth protecting, such as an industry which supports a unique culture, a strong community, or a valuable eco-system. In these contexts the social costs of removing the protection might be greater than the economic benefits.

2. It is sometimes said that **infant industries** need protection. This is an economic argument for temporary protectionism: the government of an LDC might be tempted to protect some of its manufacturers, for example, believing that until they reach a certain size they cannot compete with established manufacturers who benefit from economies of scale. On the other hand, it is argued that

the capital market should be capable of taking a view which is sufficiently long term to make protection unnecessary. As long as the long-term gains from trade outweigh the short-term costs of protectionism, an infant industry worth supporting will obtain that support, and so there is no need for the government to involve itself in 'picking winners'.

3. At the other end of the life-cycle of businesses, there are some **declining industries** for which a protection argument can be made. In the MDCs these include textiles and deep mining for coal, in the LDCs they include the production of hemp and sisal, whose markets have been invaded by man-made products. The social costs of declining industries, which include unemployment, might tempt governments to try to support such industries through protection from international competition. This denies consumers the opportunity to purchase these products at world prices. Many economists argue that the social costs are more efficiently reduced by 'targeting', that is by subsidising the industries affected.

4. **Dumping** is a practice which sometimes leads to calls for protection and occurs when foreign producers sell goods in domestic markets at below the cost of production. Theory of the firm tells us that this is a short-run phenomenon, and it is indeed usually explained by disposal of surpluses, the end of a production run, or the establishment of a brand identity. It is most likely during recessions. Dumping is harmful, especially when it is done by large multinationals in small markets with local producers, and for this reason GATT was willing to allow temporary departures from its freer trade ambitions to deal with it.

The difficulty with dumping is in establishing what the level of production cost really is. Suppose a manufacturing firm in an LDC finds that if it doubles its output of men's suits it can benefit from economies of scale, and so increase its profit margin on each suit sold. It might find that it does not have the market locally for the extra production, and so will divert the extra suits onto the export market at prices which only just cover costs. These prices could well be extremely low when compared with prices charged by manufacturers in MDCs, due to the lower labour costs. This might not technically be dumping in the strict sense of selling below the costs of production, but the prices might be so low as to lead to this impression. Local consumers, of course, will not complain about low-priced imports.

Picking tea in Rwanda. A country where tea is a significant export could find its terms of trade deteriorating.

In fact, they will welcome them – unless, of course, they find themselves out of a job as a result. The problem here is to distinguish between dumping and the legitimate selling of goods at a lower price which reflects lower costs. Footballs sewn by children in Bangladesh are cheaper than UK footballs because of low labour costs, but the cheap labour argument merges into MDC arguments that some types of competition are unfair, morally questionable and therefore justify protectionism.

The terms of trade

The **terms of trade index** is calculated from the ratio of export prices to import prices. If the prices on world markets of a country's exports rise more quickly (or fall more slowly) than its import prices, then this signifies an improvement in the terms of trade. It means that a given quantity of exports can be exchanged for a greater quantity of imports.

The terms of trade can make life difficult for countries when they have to face world trends over which they have no control. For example, in the 1970s, the increase in the world price of oil engineered by the Organisation of Oil Exporting Countries (OPEC) moved the terms of trade in favour of the oil exporters (mostly in the Middle East) and against the oil importers (including the UK). As the UK gradually became an oil exporter by exploiting the North Sea during the 1970s, the terms of trade moved back in favour of Britain, at least to some extent. It is generally assumed that the terms of trade of LDCs largely depend on the terms of trade for primary products (commodities), and that there is a tendency for the terms of trade to deteriorate, since primary products do not hold the same value as manufactures. Take as an extreme example an African or Asian country whose only significant export is tea, and which imports virtually everything else. It is likely to find its terms of trade deteriorating. This is because the price of tea rises only very slowly on world markets, and might even fall, while the price of everything else rises much more quickly. This country therefore has to export more and more tea to pay for its imports of everything else.

The General Agreement on Tariffs and Trade (GATT) and the World Trade Organisation (WTO)

The **General Agreement on Tariffs and Trade (GATT)** was one of three institutions set up in the wake of the Bretton Woods Agreements of 1944 as part of the Anglo-American grand design for post war economic development, the other two being the International Monetary Fund (IMF) and the International Fund for Reconstruction and Development (IBRD), which together are known as the 'World Bank'.

GATT was signed in Geneva in 1947 by 23 countries, and its membership steadily grew to well over 100. Finally on January 1st 1995 it was replaced by the **World Trade Organisation**, which has taken over the task of encouraging trade liberalisation.

Since the Second World War world trade has increased forty-eight fold in terms of value, and twelve fold in terms of volume. Many economists believe that this remarkable increase has been due, at least in part, to the trade liberalisation which has taken place through the eight 'rounds' of multinational trade negotiations (MTNs) which have taken place under the auspices of GATT. Each was larger and more successful than the last. The eighth round, the Uruguay Round, started in 1986 and was completed in 1994, some four years later than planned. During the round it is estimated that tariffs among industrialised countries fell from about ten per cent to 3.7 per cent, but the agenda was much wider, including such things as intellectual property rights and services as well as trade in goods. The debt crisis, the collapse of the Soviet Union, the enlargement of the EU and the creation of trade blocs in North and South America, and South East Asia raised new questions as the talks proceeded. The WTO's more recent round of negotiations (the 'Doha' round) has proceeded in fits and starts, dogged not only by anti-globalisation riots in its venue cities, but also by attempts by the LDC members to adjust their balance of power with the MDCs.

An important principle of GATT, continued by the WTO, is that of **multilateralism**, a term used to refer to trade between more than two countries, without any discrimination against particular countries. The opposite of multilateralism is **bilateralism**, or trade between two countries which necessarily involves discrimination if privileges are given which are denied to other countries. For example, Australia and Malaysia give preferential treatment to each others' products in the home market: Malaysian tin and rubber avoid protectionism in Australia in return for the same concession for Australian wheat in Malaysia. The **Most Favoured Nation** (MFN) rule which GATT members signed up to meant that any agreement of this sort would be extended to all other GATT members. Signatories to a trade treaty who offer each other favourable trading terms (such as tariff reductions) must then offer them to any other country.

While multilateralism is generally accepted as a 'good thing' which will encourage trade and hence increase economic welfare generally, the LDCs have had suspicions that its effect might be to strengthen the already strong and weaken the already weak. They have been particularly critical of the MFN clause, and they have been allowed some exemptions from it.

The WTO in practice

While most economists and politicians in positions of influence support the main principles of the WTO, there have been some criticisms to the effect that it over-represents the position of stronger countries (in effect it is dominated by the USA) and follows too uncritically the agenda of large companies (in effect American multinational enterprises). It is argued that slavish devotion to WTO rules can undermine the idea of **sustainable development**. This was manifested, for instance, in the conduct of the 'banana wars' between the USA and Europe, when attempts to protect the livelihoods of smaller producers appeared to be undermined by WTO regulations. There have also been strong indications that attempts to resist some very dubious products (such as hormone-treated meat and dairy products) on health and environmental grounds might fall foul of the WTO. American agribusiness companies have also been attempting to persuade the WTO that European health concerns about their GM products, and an insistence on clear product labelling, were in some way against the principles of free trade. A parallel development was the Multilateral Agreement on Investment (MAI), which was not concluded, but which could have seriously impaired, on very dubious 'free trade' grounds, the capacity of individual countries to improve the quality of their environmental legislation. An equally worrying development within the WTO is the insistence of some US firms that they should be allowed the right to compete with government departments for the provision of public services. This is an argument which, if accepted, could force a privatisation agenda onto a reluctant Europe, where the social model is far more concerned with communitarian values than with American-style individualism. Unlike the USA, the EU spends about 40% of its national income on public services and social welfare, and using the idea of 'free trade' to undermine the freedom of choice of Europeans to prioritise their spending in this way would be ironic, to say the least. The impact of globalisation on the public sector is further discussed in Chapter 15.

Chapter 12

Globalisation and inward investment: false friends?

Inward investment: the high point of globalisation?

As globalisation has accelerated, so have flows of Foreign Direct Investment (FDI) around the world. Ever since the days of its empire, Britain has invested overseas. Britain's outward foreign direct international investment position with the rest of the world amounts to net assets of approximately a trillion pounds. In recent years, however, Britain has become a recipient of inward investment from large multinational enterprises, and this trend has been especially important in the regions of Britain seeking new industries to replace those in decline, such as coal-mining, steel production, textiles and shipbuilding. In the early years of the Twenty First Century net inward foreign direct investment in the UK from the rest of the world approached £100 bn., and 'inward investment' had become a major policy for economic development, especially in the regions. Wales, for example, became the country with the highest concentration of Japanese firms outside Japan itself. This trend was encouraged by the UK government as a means of reducing unemployment, and was welcomed by Japanese and American and other non-European enterprise as providing a production base inside the Common External Tariff of the EU with its large single market.

While it is Japanese electronics companies such as Sony that receive most of the publicity, other 'Tiger' economies of the Pacific Rim such as Korea have invested in the UK, with names such as LG and Hyundai. Japanese car makers such as Toyota and Nissan are often referred to as the 'trailblazers' from the 1980s, but it is equally often forgotten that the true trailblazers were American firms such as Ford, General Motors and 3M, and these enterprises have been in the UK for decades. In fact, of the twenty or thirty countries that can be identified being major exporters of jobs to the UK, the largest amount of employment from foreign companies in the UK comes from the USA.

In 2003 the Harvard economist Michael Porter wrote a report for the Department of Trade and Industry arguing that other EU countries are now competing more strongly. Other economists such as John Lovering of Cardiff University were already arguing that inward investment was over-hyped, and that headline figures put forward by Conservative and Labour governments to prove the attractiveness of their low tax economies with flexible labour markets were misleading. Official announcements from Regional Development Agencies often refer to 'jobs safeguarded' as well as 'jobs created' by grants disbursed to major inward investors, and such terminology is vague enough to ensure that it is often difficult to prove or disprove a direct link between inward investment and higher levels of employment. Attention is seldom drawn to the fact that *foreign disinvestment* can take place, and that the net number of jobs created on an annual basis can be negative. This was particularly evident after the crisis in the East Asian 'Tiger' economies which took place in 1997, and which is discussed below. It was also evident during the credit crunch and recession of 2008 onwards.

The loss of inward investment jobs often means that public money has been wasted. The single biggest inward investment project anywhere in history was the LG electronics plant in South Wales. The company received a reputed £250m from government funds before it announced that it was closing its Newport plant.

Regional development agencies that have learnt the lessons of inward investment are likely to concentrate in the future on small-scale, high quality individual projects, rather than huge large-scale manufacturing facilities. Large-scale manufacturing investments are now much more likely to go to the far east, to China or other parts of Asia, where wages are lower; and if they come to the EU are likely to go to countries like Romania and Poland, for the same reason. Together with some significant dis-investment (factory closures) ordered from head offices overseas, this has made the technocrats inhabiting economic development

circles in places like Wales and Scotland go very quiet recently about their 'achievements' in attracting inward investment.

It is argued in Chapter 18, the future for Britain lies in adding value and innovation, rather than mass production at low cost. It is also argued that Britain's isolation from the euro will become an increasingly important barrier to long term investment.

The collapse of the tigers: a low point of globalisation

During the credit crunch and recession that closed the first decade of the Twenty-First Century, many economists expressed surprise at the turn of events, and many politicians claimed that the crash was 'unprecedented'. It is therefore instructive to recall that just over a decade earlier there was a regionalised example of rapid, speculative growth, financial collapse and recession, which should have served as a warning about the dangers of unregulated financial markets.

During the 1980s and 1990s economists and politicians in the UK looked to the newly-industrialised countries known as the 'Asian Tigers' as role models. While the British still struggled to become as European in outlook as their nearest neighbours, British leaders readily accepted that the far-away Pacific Rim was where it was all happening, and even took it upon themselves to lecture their EU colleagues on the virtues of East Asian mantras such as 'flexible labour markets'. British trade unionists attended symposia on how their members can compete with the 'challenge' of the Tigers. A senior Conservative even advocated Britain becoming an 'Atlantic Singapore', channelling trade between Europe and the world. As mentioned above, UK development agencies tripped over each other in their enthusiasm to import East Asian capital from South Korea's LG, with Wales finally winning the battle at a reputed cost of some £250 million or £40,000 per job. Before their ascent to power New Labour politicians spent some time in Australia, not only wooing the Murdoch media chiefs, but also observing how Australian politicians forged relationships with the Tiger economies. While Irish politicians have been more than happy to hear their country described as the 'Celtic Tiger', policy makers in Poland have staked their claim to the Eastern European version of the same title.

What exactly is a 'Tiger Economy'? What was the secret of their success? Why, during the summer of 1997, did everything seem to go wrong? What are the lessons to be learned?

Singapore, Hong Kong, Taiwan and South Korea belonged to an elite of countries. Throughout the 1960s and 70s their average growth rates were at least 6% of GNP, and during the 1980s and 90s were even higher. By contrast the New Labour government and the Bank of England believe that growth rates above 4% are 'unsustainable' in the UK. Furthermore, in the developed world, unemployment continued to be a persistent problem (although politicians have had difficulties in defining and measuring it) whereas it was rare to find a Tiger politician who would admit to the problem existing at all; many claimed that in their culture they do not even understand the concept.

Why were the Tigers so successful? Here is a ten-point sketch.

1. They were held to have gained success by the use of free enterprise in unfettered markets. Close inspection does reveal, however, that governments played a crucial role. In politics the Tigers are hardly paragons of democracy and they are often accused of severe repression. In the economic sphere government action has been vigorous but has, on the whole, been designed not to replace markets but to enable market forces to operate more freely. This type of **market-friendly government intervention** has been described as '**state capitalism**'. Some observers claim that state capitalism is as much a part of the Tiger business culture as Confuscianism is a part of the general outlook on life, and that cultural attitudes, such as respect for authority, supremacy of collective objectives over the individual, and a willingness to wait patiently for long-term returns are a natural part of East Asian general social values.

Singapore is one of the 'Tiger Economies'.

2. In the absence of natural factor endowments, the four Tigers placed **great emphasis on investment in human capital**. The roots of Tony Blair's phrase about 'education, education and education' in 1997, shortly before he became British Prime Minister, can be traced directly to the priorities of the Tigers and their belief that education and training have powerful economic returns.

3. Growth in the Tigers was **export-led**, seeking the advantages of free trade in a global market.

4. The citizens of the Tiger economies have traditionally had **high savings ratios**, indeed higher than anywhere else in the world (over 40% of GDP). It is no accident that when he was Chancellor of the Exchequer Gordon Brown said that he had adopted an aim of shifting Britain from consumption to saving, and from expenditure to investment. New Labour theorists, seeking a way out of the pensions time-tomb, have cast envious glances at Singapore's methods of enforced saving as an alternative to state provision.

5. The Tigers participated fully in the de-regulation of financial markets, and in so doing made **full use of foreign capital**.

6. Exchange rates, however, were not generally allowed to float. Instead, Tiger governments preferred to try to peg their currencies to the US dollar. This provided stability and enabled long-term planning.

7. Where necessary, external sources of money was borrowed to finance investment, particularly from Japanese financial institutions.

8. They diversified and entered new markets, for example using Japanese technology to make mass-produced cars for export.

9. Full use was made of economies of scale. Instead of relying on small local markets, Tiger companies produced and sold their output globally.

10. Finally, market forces were unleashed on their labour markets, which became a by-word for 'flexibility', which in effect meant fewer trade union rights, lower wages and greater uncertainty for the employee; and the power to hire and fire for the employer.

These features were adopted by 'copycat' Tigers, notably Thailand, Malaysia and Indonesia, eager to join the club. And not only in Africa and Latin America, but even in the developed world, economists and politicians came to believe that in order to compete they had to look the Tigers straight in the eye and adapt to their ways.

But then what happened? In the summer of 1997, a series of crises rocked the by now widely-held assumptions. In July, the King of Thailand summoned his Prime Minister to the palace to explain why the Baht had taken a dive against other currencies, losing about 40% of its value. This was the curtain raiser for a three-month financial pummelling whereby stock-markets throughout East Asia underwent what has been called euphemistically a 'correction'. In reality it placed this part of the world in a position which is embarrassingly familiar elsewhere: politicians having to go cap in hand to the IMF in order to seek financial bail-outs. With the Korean Won on the slide, falling by 50% against the dollar, the regime there had to ask for a record $20 billion loan from the IMF, while analysts suggested that five times that amount would eventually be needed. And it goes without saying that any assistance from this quarter tends to have conditions attached that ensure even more use of free markets, even less social provision, and even more flexible labour markets.

In Britain, during the summer of 1997, there was remarkably little analysis of the reasons for the hiatus in Tiger finances. It was as if British observers were in denial and could not accept that our newly discovered role models had been found wanting. Perhaps there was a lurking fear of the analysis that dare not speak its name. Perhaps Keynes was right all along, perhaps unregulated free markets are inherently unstable. Perhaps the new economic orthodoxy, so readily embraced by New Labour among others, was fatally flawed. Could it be that a world of low taxes, individualised wage bargaining, and government disengagement from social provision – as envisaged by the IMF, the World Bank, the EU's convergence criteria and Growth and Stability Pact, the Bank of England and the Treasury – was a deflationary, high interest rate, low wage world that was safe for its bankers and grand multinationals, but not for its workaday manufacturers, service providers and ordinary citizens?

To begin with, the Old World media presented the crisis as a sort of hiccup in the financial markets, almost a purely monetary problem, hardly connected at all to the real world of producing, selling, working and earning. But due to their proximity to the economies in turmoil, the perspective from the New World was rather different, and real-economy effects were felt more quickly.

For example an Australian university reported in September 1997 that its enrolment of foreign students (nearly all Asian) for the January intake was 30% down, because many had seen family businesses wiped out by the weight of foreign currency loans and collapsing exchange rates. It was not until early 1998 that universities in the UK such as Manchester University began to report problems because of their reliance on overseas students whose grants were being withdrawn by Tiger governments. At car boot sales in Bangkok, redundant executives tried to shift bottles of Chateau Mouton Rothschild, Mercedes cars and even Cessna two-seat aircraft! In a desperate attempt to clear land quickly for cash crops to generate hard currency earnings, forest burning caused regional smoke pollution. This was the alleged cause of a serious airline accident; this in turn has hit the local tourist industry, and many major companies in the area began to face ruin.

These cases were but the tip of an iceberg. It used to be said that 'when the USA sneezed, Europe caught a cold'. In the late 1990s business and political leaders throughout the developed world had to brace themselves for a bout of 'Pacific flu' which threatened to affect not just the world of the money-shifters but the real economy as well. However, it is important not to suggest that all East Asian economies are the same. The economies of Hong Kong and Singapore, for example, appeared to be built on rather more solid foundations than the rest, and showed signs of weathering the crisis better.

The collapse of major Japanese banks after being accused of being connected with organised crime and concealed debts added further storm clouds over what was supposed to have been the Century of the

Pacific. Luckily for the UK, the investments received from Japanese and Tiger companies tend to be not the paper assets of stocks and bonds, but the real type of productive assets which cannot so quickly be withdrawn. One very positive aspect of Pacific business culture is the willingness to take a long term view of investments in real assets. In the short term, their owners wished, if anything, to work these assets even harder to help repay debt; but as time went on global recessionary effects from Pacific financial crashes tended to negate this wish by depressing demand. In the short run, then, western consumers experienced a mini-bonanza of cheap videos, cars and other Tiger products, and benefited from the anti-inflationary effects that these bargain prices created. In the longer run the Tiger collapse became deflationary in the sense of depressing world demand and causing unemployment.

What went wrong with the Tigers? Here is a ten-point answer.

1. These economies were non-Keynesian in the sense of attempting to influence the level of economic activity or redistribute wealth (except from the less well-off to the better off)...

2. ...but they were very interventionist in establishing what many would see as inappropriate industry, for example Indonesia's aircraft industry, Malaysia's car plant, and skyscrapers (which are half empty) everywhere.

3. Most of these industries depended on foreign currency loans...

4. ...and many were run by cronies of the power elites and were uncompetitive without large amounts of protection.

5. Central banks in the Tigers had all tried to hold domestic currencies to the US dollar. Ostensibly this provided stability for everyone, but incidentally protected foreign currency borrowers (often the government itself).

6. Large government debt was used to fund rapid infrastructure growth, often crony built and operated at inflated contract prices. Aid assisted projects like the Pergau Dam had dubious economic and environmental benefits.

7. Monopolies were government protected. For example in Indonesia flour was estimated to be 30% overpriced because only certain people (allegedly friends and relatives of the president) had the licence to mill it.

8. Asset inflation was built on debt. In Hong Kong for instance the Hang Seng index had risen at twice the rate of the (already inflated) Dow Jones since 1991; property price rises had been even higher.

9. In essence, a variety of non-viable, non-returning investments built on debt in foreign currencies and repayments supported only by domestic currencies kept artificially high by their own central banks and reducing their export competitiveness.

10. One or two significant loan repayments were missed, and in moved the currency speculators and the IMF, as any college student of development economics worth their salt could have predicted.

All this plus the environmental catastrophe caused by the fires lit by plantation companies clearing jungle all over South East Asia. The citizens of Kuala Lumpur did not see the sun for three months. Even in the Northern Territory of Australia light planes were grounded by smoke. Also, there was the social disaster that was likely to result from some of the governments deciding to re-trench by expelling migrant workers. The spin-off effects of such action in both Less Developed Countries and their developed trading partners were a serious cause for concern.

What were the lessons for the UK?

In our enthusiasm for inward investment as the Holy Grail of economic development, perhaps we could have paused to reflect on the importance of *culture*. Dr. Peter Smith of Southampton University has drawn

attention to the fact that whether we mean business, political or social culture, its role in economic development is all too often overlooked. Authoritarian government and devil-take-the-hindmost market forces might be more compatible with some general cultures than with others. Whether a country has a history of Confuscianism or Methodism, for example, might make it better or less prepared for the unleashing of individualistic market forces, or might make its population more or less liable to support the democratic and communitarian values of public service.

Perhaps we needed to be a bit more 'choosy' when selecting our role models. We could envy the priority that the Tigers appeared to give to such things as entrepreneurial flair and investment in infrastructure and education. But we can also appreciate the dangers of unsocialised markets and unaccountable government.

If at some time in the future Britain re-discovers a devolutionist mission, so that power is dispersed from appointed agencies to elected assemblies in its regions (as has already happened in Wales, Scotland, London and Northern Ireland) it might be that we can move towards a development policy that is more open, transparent and accountable. This could help to ensure that the economic results of inward investment are more sustainable in the long run.

In 2007, shortly before it became clear that the credit crunch would lead to a full recession, Joseph Stiglitz marked the tenth anniversary of the Asia financial crisis by saying that two important lessons had still not been learned. The first was that, without adequate safeguards, the opening up of the financial markets of developing countries is dangerous, and that the risks were being disguised or even hidden by hedge funds and secret bank accounts. The second was that in an integrated, globalised world, there is a need for strong international institutions that enhance stability.

In 2009, when it was all too clear that the credit crunch had led to a deep recession, Gordon Brown was reported to have said 'sorry' for his role in the banking failures that caused the global recession and declared that the era of *laissez faire* government was over. He said that it should have been recognised sooner that the national system of bank regulation that he helped establish in 1997 was too weak to keep pace with massive global financial flows. He was reported as saying that after the Asian crisis of 1997, when many countries assumed these problems would just go away, Britain should have been tougher in bringing issues of stricter regulation onto the international agenda.

Brown's comments can be interpreted as an attempt to make a partial apology while simultaneously attempting to deflect blame onto the global economy, in other words to try to convince people that nobody was specifically to blame. The fact cannot be escaped, however, that only months before the credit crunch, British ministers such as Peter Mandelson were still complaining that 'over-regulation' was harming the 'competitiveness' of the British financial sector, and throughout the decade from 1997 to 2007, the UK government resisted pressure from building societies and smaller banks for laws to help protect them from being swallowed up by larger corporations. Many mutual societies owned by their savers rather than by shareholders, were forced by demands from investors looking for quick short-term profits to turn themselves into limited companies owned by shareholders. During the horrors of the credit crunch, those building societies that had resisted pressure and remained as mutuals survived the crisis, mainly because their capital portfolios consisted of real assets like bricks and mortar and the savings of their members, rather than the speculative paper assets owned by the majority of the banking sector. Meanwhile, not a single de-mutualised financial institution survived intact. They all lost their individual identities as parts of larger commercial banks, and then in effect became part of the state sector being bailed out by the taxpayer. They had, in the government's newly-enlightened view, become 'too big to fail'.

At the level of industrial policy, the lessons of the Tigers' collapse were certainly not learned in the UK, least of all the dangers of putting too much faith in the financial sector, too much reliance on inflationary property values, too little thought being given to the regulation of the banks, while at the same time giving too low a priority to manufacturing and other aspects of the real economy. We return to this theme in Chapter 18.

Chapter 13

Why are some countries in debt?

International saving, investing and borrowing

Most developed countries are able to finance their own investments from their own saving. There is such a thing as a 'development trap', which describes a cycle of poverty where low income leads to low saving, low saving leads to low investment, and low investment leads in turn to low income. If a country wishes to invest more than it saves, then it can look beyond its borders for flows of money. These flows can come in three main forms: **foreign direct investment** (FDI), **borrowing**, or **aid** (discussed in Chapter 14).

Foreign direct investment

The importance of FDI as part of the phenomenon of globalisation was discussed in Chapter 12. Flows of international investment mostly pass from one MDC (More Developed Country) to another; and while FDI as a whole has risen dramatically since the 1990s, and flows from MDCs to LDCs (Less Developed Countries) have increased, the amounts received by LDCs have not risen as steeply. Certain LDCs, such as some rapidly-growing economies in Latin America, received a much bigger amount of inward investment during the 1990s than poorer economies such as those of, say, sub-Saharan Africa.

Borrowing

(a) From international institutions

The **IMF** has an important role in exchange rate adjustment, and it also acts as a lending institution. IMF lending was originally intended to overcome temporary balance of payments difficulties, but in the 1970s and 80s, due to the end of the Bretton Woods system of fixed exchange rates, the oil price rise, and the problems of LDC debt, the amount and the role of IMF lending was extended. The *conditionality* of this lending is sometimes controversial because fund loans were accompanied by programmes of measures agreed with the recipient country. This means that the IMF has had a great deal of influence over economic policies all over the world, particularly in the LDCs, where a Fund programme is often seen as a seal of approval, giving access to further investment from other international organisations, and from private sector banks and multinational enterprises.

In the early 1980s, many World Bank loans, in similar fashion to IMF loans were made conditional on the recipient country adopting certain economic policies known as **structural adjustment**, mainly directed towards the encouragement of private enterprise and removal of trade barriers. These policies forced the recipient government to agree to a significant degree of privatisation, and this was particularly controversial when applied to basic public services and utilities such as the supply of water. In effect, low company taxes, together with job insecurity, low wages, and a cutback of social safety nets became the unwritten consequences of the IMF/World Bank world view.

(b) From banks: the LDC debt problem

Another kind of debt is commercial debt, so called because it is raised from private commercial banks. The debt crisis of the 1980s was largely caused by the expansion of commercial debt, and can now be considered an historical event from which powerful lessons needed to be drawn. During the late 1970s and early 1980s it became clear that a number of LDCs, particularly in Latin America, were no longer able to maintain **debt servicing**, in other words they were unable to repay either the capital sum borrowed or the interest payments.

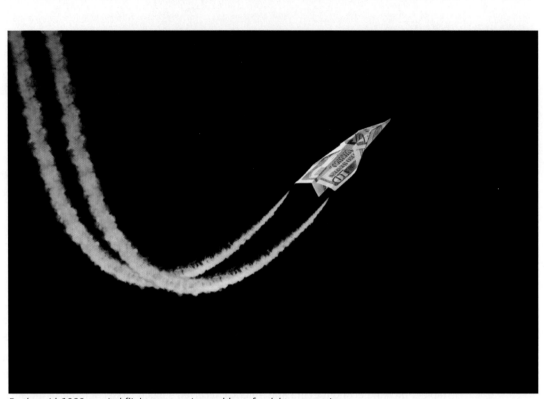

By the mid-1980s capital flight was causing problems for debtor countries.

A fundamental principle of good banking practice is that business loans should be made to enterprises which have a good chance of repaying the loans through their future business activities. Loans should not be made in order to service previous debts. These principles were largely forgotten by commercial banks in the 1980s when they fell over themselves to lend to LDCs. The commercial banks thus stood accused of imprudence, and of reacting to the deregulation of financial markets over-enthusiastically to say the least. In some cases, money was lent to finance projects with little chance of producing income-generating goods and services, simply because they were poor business projects whose future profitability had not been properly appraised. In other cases the money was used corruptly by the recipients, or not invested for business purposes at all. In some countries loans were dissipated on military expenditure, either for possible use against a potentially unfriendly neighbouring country, or even more probably for use by dictators against their own citizens. Western financial institutions have been particularly criticised for lending money to certain projects damming rivers on a huge scale with severe human and environmental consequences. Projects of this sort in China are displacing millions of people.

One of the most infamous episodes occurred in 1982 when Mexico announced that it could no longer service its external debt. Similar news from Brazil (1987) and Argentina came soon afterwards. Major banks began to write off billions of dollars from their company accounts due to non-repayment of loans to Latin America. In doing so the LDC debt crisis had begun.

In many cases, the debt crisis of LDCs reflected unforeseen changes in the economic environment for both lender and borrower. Loans were taken out by oil exporters like Mexico and Venezuela when oil was riding high in the late 1970s at over $40 a barrel, but in 1986 the price collapsed to below $30 a barrel. In the late 1970s, the exports and real incomes of LDCs as a whole were rising at an annual rate of around 10%; but due to world recession they were declining in real terms in the early 1980s. When Argentina's inflation rate rose from 30% to 3000% per year, and when interest rates in Brazil and Chile rose from 10% to 20%, debts became that much more difficult to service. From 1980 to 1982, the export earnings of all LDCs fell by $80 billion or 15%, while their annual interest rate bill rose from $31 billion to $46 billion, an increase of 48%. The LDCs now proved to be casualties of the adoption of new right wing monetarist policies in Britain and the USA from 1980. As the rate of interest became the central weapon of domestic macroeconomic management under the Thatcher and Reagan governments in the early 1980s, floating rate debt taken out by LDCs experienced a virtual doubling of interest rates between 1978 and 1983. Where countries were unable to service their debts due to rising interest rates, they borrowed more and more just to pay off past debts. Thus the debt crisis was to some extent a result of the experiment with monetarism.

Measuring the extent of indebtedness is difficult, but a good benchmark is that any country with outstanding debts worth more than 200 per cent of the value of its exports is in difficulty. An alternative would be that any country spending over 40 per cent of its export revenues on debt servicing in any year has similar difficulties. In 1986 the seventeen most heavily-indebted countries had net external indebtedness of over 380 per cent of exports. The situation was complicated by **capital flight**, meaning private capital which sped out of the LDCs and into foreign bank accounts when the debt crisis broke, of over $100 billion from 19 debtor countries between 1984 and 1987.

During the later 1980s negotiations took place to re-schedule these debts, that is to pay them over longer periods of time with reduced rates of interest. These negotiations culminated in the Brady Plan, put forward at a meeting of the Bretton Woods Committee in March 1989 by James Brady, the US Secretary for the Treasury. This plan proposed case-by-case voluntary debt-reduction by the commercial banks, with the IMF and World Bank offering resources to countries with 'viable' economic programmes.

Ten years after Mexico's dramatic announcement *The Economist* newspaper carried an article by a prominent banker describing the LDC debt crisis as 'The disaster that didn't happen'. This might be an accurate description from the point of view of the major banks, since they managed to survive the decade without one of their number failing due to LDC debt difficulties from Latin America. However it is arguable whether this view would be shared by citizens of an LDC displaced from their land by an IMF-inspired programme to produce cash crops.

Nonetheless the crisis was certainly not over for Africa. Over 30 low income countries, nearly all in Africa, owed $230 billion at the end of 1993, and although this is only 15 per cent of total LDC debt, it was four times as large as their exports. Not much of this debt is commercial debt, but much is bilateral, for example between former French colonies in West Africa and France. Recent discussions in the World Bank have focused on methods of reducing the share of repayments to multilateral agencies like themselves and the IMF.

The debt crisis has consequences for the environment. Assets with a global significance, such as South American rain forests are being cleared to produce grazing for beef cattle. As mentioned earlier, the prudent servicing of external debt involves the creation of income generating assets. This 'monetarisation' of economic life should not involve the liquidation of non-renewable resources with long-term global environmental consequences in order to overcome a short-term local problem.

It is a sad fact that while non-governmental organisations, such as voluntary relief agencies, struggle in order to provide resources for LDCs in need, official agencies do little to alter the situation where official flows of capital are actually leaving the LDCs in order to repay institutions in the west whose owners and directors are already rewarding themselves with the fruits of record profits.

The debt crisis is one which still has to be properly addressed by the richer nations. Unless radical action is taken, we will continue to observe the scandalous spectacle of poor countries exporting merely to pay previous debts, while their citizens suffer conditions at home whose existence should not be tolerated by anyone anywhere in a civilised world. Tragically, since 2008, as we discuss in Chapter 17, the indebtedness of LDCs has been eclipsed in the media of the MDCs, as politicians wrestle with the indebtedness that has now been forced upon them by the further misadventures of an under-regulated global banking system.

Chapter 14

Why is trade better than aid?

Types of aid

A question that is often asked is whether international trade is better than aid at improving living standards. The standard answer is 'yes', and most economists would agree that trade is generally better than aid. There are, however, different ways of doing trade, and different types of aid.

The word 'aid' perhaps carries suggestions of charity, but in fact covers a large number of different ways in which money and resources are given by one country to another without expecting full repayment. At one extreme is **grant aid**, where money, food aid or emergency relief are given as a gift with no repayments of any kind expected. However, gifts are only a small proportion of total aid. A large amount of aid is in the form of loans at below-market rates of interest, known as **soft loans**. Thus in broad terms, aid can be regarded as almost any subsidy aimed at encouraging economic growth. We generally think of 'aid' as something which MDCs provide for LDCs, but within MDCs, or groups of MDCs, we can also observe 'aid' taking place in the form of transfers from richer to poorer regions. Within the EU, for example, there are 'cohesion policies' aimed at bringing poorer countries up to average levels of income, and 'regional development funds', with various 'objectives' aimed at reducing regional disparities.

Aid can be official, in which case it is called **official development assistance** (ODA), and administered by governments or government agencies, or it can be unofficial, in which case it is administered by a non-governmental body such as a charity. A great deal of official aid is **tied aid**, which means that the recipient country has to agree to buy goods or services from the donor. **Multilateral aid** involves the giving of aid to international aid agencies who then decide where need is greatest. **Bilateral aid** (from one country to another) tends to follow pathways that are historical, political or cultural in origin: the UK and France sending aid to former colonies, for example, OPEC members making donations to other Arab countries, or the USA giving financial support to Israel. The result is that 40% of these aid funds flow to countries containing only 20% of the world's poor people.

Aid and controversy

As official aid has become more politicised, given with strings attached, and increasingly in the form of loans rather than grants, so there has been a growth in aid from voluntary multilateral aid agencies, otherwise known as **NGOs (non-governmental organisations)**, such as Oxfam, Cafod, Save the Children and Comic Relief. These groups have the advantage of being open, widely known (often with much higher public recognition factors than official bodies), non-ideological, and widely trusted (often more trusted than governments). The best also pride themselves on reducing bureaucratic costs to the minimum, and generally they have a reputation for targeting their funds carefully towards lasting self-help projects that help the very poorest. However, by themselves their resources will never be enough to eradicate the problems of poverty, overpopulation, disease, and lack of life chances faced by so many of the world's existing and future citizens. Ultimately, only governments acting in concert can mobilise the necessary resources.

Critics do not have to search very hard to find evidence that government aid is often misdirected, badly administered, or even used corruptly. Tied aid causes special problems, for instance in 1988 an export order for Hawk aircraft to Malaysia somehow became linked to a promise of aid towards the Pergau Dam, which was in itself a controversial project, with critics arguing that it was unnecessary and would displace populations rather than provide overall benefits. Despite attempts to keep the matter secret, the use of the aid budget to secure arms exports was subsequently ruled illegal in the High Court and deemed economically unsound by the senior civil service. Although the New Labour government professed the aim of an 'ethical foreign policy' it has not succeeded yet in removing the distinct impression that aid programmes are largely geared towards military and financial interests.

The World Bank has claimed that aid in the narrow sense of gifts, particularly food aid, has only had limited success. Food aid provides a convenient way for some countries, such as EU members, to dispose of their surpluses, which do not always match the dietary needs of the recipients, and the resulting distortions of consumption patterns tend to increase the dependency of recipients on continued food aid. However aid in the wider sense, including soft loans channelled through UN institutions, has had more success (according to the World Bank), especially where the funds are used to finance specific projects and where the recipient country organises itself so as to make efficient use of the funds received.

Third World economists are increasingly seeing the problems of the poorer countries as revolving around the unequal distribution of incomes, rather than the lack of total resources. In many so-called 'famine' situations, for example, people have starved to death in front of full granaries. What they lacked was the means to buy the food that was actually available. For this reason the claims of multinational agri-businesses that their genetically-modified organisms will one day solve the problem of feeding the world have spectacularly failed to impress.

Critics would say that institutional aid places too much faith in the now widely discredited ideas of **trickle-down theory**, is too much concentrated on large scale projects in urban and industrial sectors, and that money should be directed to the poorest in society, developing the rural areas, increasing the spending power of the poor, and generating a demand for locally produced goods.

There are those who claim, on the one hand, that without aid many LDCs would be substantially worse off than they are today. On the other hand others claim that aid is in reality a barrier to progress. Given these diverging views perhaps the most sensible conclusion to come to is that the amount of aid flowing from the MDCs to the LDCs for purely economic or commercial objectives has in fact been too small to have made much difference either way in all except the very poorest LDCs. In this sense, then, to address the question with which we started this chapter, the future lies with trade, not aid.

The trickle-down theory in now widely discredited.

Aid and development

Dependency theory suggests that countries can become over-reliant on aid, and that far from being altruistic, the aid giver has a vested interest in making donations. When young babies in Africa are given dried milk, for example, their mothers cannot suddenly switch on their own milk again when the aid ceases. Instead, they become long-term customers of certain multinational companies, locked into the products of the giant food concerns. However, it is not only in LDCs that politicians can tend to become reliant on aid rather than trade. The early proceedings of the Scottish Parliament and the Welsh Assembly tended to be dominated by discussions of regional funding from the EU. In many ways this was a pity, and it might have been better in the long run if the devolved regions of Britain were encouraged to think of themselves as dynamic, trading, exporting entities in their own right rather than as poor relations in need of handouts. Trade rather than aid is a slogan that could well be applied to the regions of Britain, as they seek to develop in a globalised world.

Chapter 15

Industry and environment: market forces or government action?

Globalised service provision?

It is often assumed that globalisation means little more than the ability for countries to trade freely in goods. What about services? On the one hand it is true that many services are, by their very nature, localised and incapable of being traded internationally. If you want a haircut, for example, you are more likely to get it done in your town's high street rather than to travel to say, Milan or New York. On the other hand, some services, such as leisure and tourism, have become more and more globalised as time has gone on. It is often claimed that Manchester United Football Club has more fans in India than it has in the UK. This is largely due to globalised markets in satellite communications and television technology. Similarly, holiday destinations such as Porthcawl, Eastbourne and Whitley Bay have been opened up to the bracing competition provided by Barcelona, Orlando and Macchu Pichu.

There is also a form of globalisation entering the market for public services. As mentioned in Chapter 11, as part of the World Trade Organisation's deliberations, some American companies are attempting to force national governments to allow them to bid for contracts to provide such things as health and education. Considering the ground given voluntarily by successive British governments, allowing multinationals to move into supply of prison services, education administration, electricity generation, and railway operation – to name but a few – it is clear that such companies are often knocking on an open door.

Does globalisation inevitably mean that market forces will rule, or is there still a role for government action?

'Market forces' is one of the most potent phrases in use in the present day. How often do we use this phrase without fully understanding what it means? Politicians sometimes say 'You can't buck the market'. Conservative politician Michael Heseltine famously used this phrase in the 1980s, and former Labour leader Tony Blair repeated it in the late 1990s. Is it true? What exactly is a 'market' and what are these mysterious 'market forces'?

In the first part of your economics course you are likely to examine what it is that markets can do, what markets are good at. It is then necessary to examine the relationship between market forces and business decisions and to look at circumstances where markets are not so useful, and where there is a strong possibility of market failure.

We are familiar with 'markets' which are places, such as the local produce market in your town. On television we often see images of market-makers working in dealing rooms, shouting prices at each other. To an economist, however, the word 'market' conveys an idea rather than a place. When we talk about 'the labour market' or the 'housing market', or the 'foreign exchange market' we are describing a network rather than a place. This is a network of dealings, making it possible for buyers to buy and sellers to sell. True, there are places we can go to in order to buy and sell houses, for instance, but when we ask 'what is the state of the housing market?' we are speaking about markets in the abstract. And even though it is tied to a geographical area, namely Europe, the single market is an idea – the idea that trade can take place without international barriers. So a market is a set of arrangements which enables the buyers of a good or service (or the consumers) to strike a deal with the sellers (or the producers) of the good or service. In economic terminology, a market brings together the supply of a product and the demand for a product.

Why are markets important? Consider a simple product, such as the implement – probably a ball-point pen – which you use to make lesson notes. How did this pen arrive in your possession? Almost certainly, markets had a prominent part in the process. Think of all the 'ingredients' that go into a ball-point pen.

The plastic in the body of the pen is manufactured from oil, which ultimately can be traced back to a source in the North Sea or in the Middle East. The metal in its nib may come from Asia or the Americas. The ink is a chemical compound which may be manufactured in, say, France, from raw materials shipped from Africa. When you go into your newsagents because you need a new pen, you will find hundreds of pens, ready and waiting for you to choose from amongst them. How did they get there? How were resources organised to get all the raw materials together so that pens were provided at a price you could afford? Why did companies set themselves up and make it their business to get a pen to you, available at a time and place and at a price convenient to you? How was the price decided upon? How was it decided that all the effort that went into producing and transporting your pen was worth a price of just a few pence, as opposed to hundreds of pounds? The answer to these questions can be summed up by the phrase 'market forces'.

Market failure, government failure

The idea of a 'perfect market' assumes a minimum amount of government intervention in the economy. However in reality all economies are 'mixed' to some extent, in that there is no such thing as a purely planned economy, nor is there such a thing as a complete free-market economy with no government intervention. Even in the western democracies traditionally described as mixed economies there has been a fierce debate about the degree of planning and the extent to which prices should be freely determined.

The strongest case for government intervention in the micro-economy arises from **market failure**. Market failure occurs for three reasons widely known to economists. Firstly, there is the resource misallocation that stems from any departure from perfect competition and the fact that monopolists seek to dominate markets and exploit consumers. Secondly, there is the slowness of markets to react to disequilibrium. Workers made redundant by the failure of one industry, for example, need government support during their transition period of retraining and seeking work in an alternative sector. Thirdly, there are externalities. As economic development takes place there is bound to be an increase in both the production and consumption of goods and services. Production and consumption both involve the creation of costs and benefits, and these costs and benefits can be internal or private (experienced only by the individual producer or consumer), or they can be external or public (side effects experienced not only by the producer or consumer, but also by the community at large). So the full costs to society (social costs) of any act of production or consumption will consist of both the private costs and the public side effects, which could be positive or negative.

Welfare economists suggest that efficiency and welfare are increased if negative externalities are taxed (for example the polluter pays principle) and positive externalities are subsidised (for example, free primary education). These actions 'internalise' the externalities, and so force the producer or consumer to consider the full social costs (or benefits) of their actions. Thus a firm polluting a river, for example, and relying on the taxpayer to pay for its dirty work, could be forced by taxation to reflect the pollution costs in higher prices and/or lower profits.

Environmental policy

Environmental problems are global, by their very nature, and the 'polluter pays' idea is one which today receives a great deal of support (in principle at least) from economists and politicians alike. Another concept which is becoming increasingly important to economists is that of **sustainable development**.

In 1987 the UN World Commission on Environment and Development (the *Brundtland Commission*) defined sustainable development as development that meets the needs of the present without compromising the ability of future generations to meet their own needs.

We are likely to find that political debate and economic policy will increasingly focus on this idea of sustainable development. The global consumer economy will need to be examined critically, and intergovernmental action will be needed to ensure that the priorities of the multinational enterprises correspond with the best interests of the majority of world citizens. The full cost, that is the social cost (including internalities and externalities) of producing goods and services and consuming resources and creating externalities will have to be built into prices. Markets and governments will have to work in harmony to achieve this; neither can achieve it in isolation. Neither will individual governments be effective on their own; action will have to be international.

This is, in effect, an argument for *increased* government action. However, the fashion for *reducing* the role of government to uncover the profit-seeking instincts of the private sector has spread throughout the world in the 1990s. For example, there had been over 800 privatisations of substantial state assets in the world by 1995, many of them supervised by the British merchant banks who pioneered the sale of huge utilities such as British Telecom and British Gas in the 1980s.

As well as the possibility of market failure there exists the possibility of what is known as **government failure** – a less than optimal pattern of output arising from political preferences that differ from consumer preferences. The choice facing a globalised world is not one between perfect markets and imperfect governments; nor is it one between perfect governments and imperfect markets. It is a case of finding the best balance between markets and governments, both of which are bound to be imperfect.

For the foreseeable future it appears that global warming, or what politicians now prefer to refer to as **climate change** will dominate the political agenda. It appears that, with some notable exceptions, scientists around the world are agreed that human activity is having potentially disastrous effects on the environment, which call for strong programmes to reduce emissions of carbon dioxide. From an economist's point of view, there are two types of policy that can be used.

Firstly, *command and control methods*. These include directives, limits and bans on certain activities. International action was taken, for example, to ban chemicals called CFCs as propellants in aerosols and coolants in refrigerators, as these were believed to be contributing to damage to the ozone layer. Restrictions on the number of take-offs and landings at airports, and regulations on emissions from car engines are further examples. One major problem with command and control methods is that they need policing, and another is that universal international agreement and enforcement is necessary. But a major advantage is that they will work quickly *if enforced*.

Secondly, there are *market-based methods*, such as carbon trading schemes, where industries buy permits to pollute, which give a financial incentive to firms that adopt non-polluting technology. Other examples include taxation on polluting activities, such as the airport departure tax, and the road pricing schemes, such as the central London congestion charge. The advantage of such methods is that they help internalise externalities, and the 'polluter pays' a price closer to the true social cost of their economic activity. A disadvantage is that polluters might choose to pay rather than reduce their polluting, and another is that governments might be reluctant to increase environmental taxes enough to stamp out the polluting activity, as they may become dependent on the tax revenue that it raises. Also, again, international action is necessary, otherwise the polluting activity will simply move to a low tax region of the global economy. This argument is used to explain why petrol for cars is heavily taxed, whereas the even more highly polluting aviation fuel is tax free.

The nearly 200 countries whose representatives attended the United Nations summit conference on climate change, which took place in Copenhagen in December 2009, found it very difficult to reconcile the environmental concerns of small maritime countries and less developed continental countries, on the one hand, with those of the already industrialised world on the other.

From the point of view of a citizen of the UK, the mobilisation of public opinion in favour of carbon reduction programmes was made difficult by mixed messages from politicians and contradictory government policies. Nearly all the high-ranking politicians at Copenhagen arrived at the conference by air and some were on record as supporting the controversial third runway at London Heathrow Airport.

Politicians who at home argued for more energy to be produced at coal-fired power stations were arguing for carbon reduction at Copenhagen. Consumers at home could be forgiven for thinking that replacing their light bulbs with a low energy version at the family level would be an insignificant and futile act in comparison with large scale pollution taking place at the industrial level with government blessing and support.

Table 15.1: Public goods, mixed goods, private goods

Main Features	Type of Good		
	Public Good	**Mixed Good (Merit/Demerit)**	**Private Good**
Examples ...	National defence, law and order, public health, (e.g. sanitation) light-houses	Health (hospital treatment), education, buses, trains, roads	TV sets, clothes, baked beans, cars, cornflakes, etc. etc.
Diminishability/ Rivalry ...	Non-diminishable/ Non-rival	Diminishable/ rivalrous	Diminishable/ rivalrous
Excludability ...	Non-excludable	Excludable: but society decides that as many people as possible should be encouraged to be included (merit goods); or that the price mechanism by itself does not sufficiently discourage use (demerit goods)	Excludable
Benefits ...	Communal (mainly positive externalities)	Individual and communal. *Merit goods:* strong positive externalities (those included share benefits with others). *Demerit goods:* strong negative externalities (those included impose costs on others)	Individual (mainly internalities)
Provider ...	Usually, but not necessarily, the government	The government and/or private enterprise	Usually, but not necessarily, private enterprise
Financed by ...	Usually taxation (the 'ability to pay' principle)	Taxes and/or prices	Usually through the price system (the 'beneficial' principle)

Public goods and privatisation

Public goods, merit goods and natural monopolies are important topics in economics. Even in free market economies, state intervention is often found in the provision of **public goods**. These are best provided by the state because they are:

- *non-excludable* (individuals cannot be stopped from consuming them), and
- *non-diminishable* (one person's use does not deprive another).

Examples are national defence, law and order, and public health measures (such as clean air and the eradication of infectious diseases). Provision at all means provision for all, and it is unlikely that their provision could be achieved by any supplier other than the state, which has access through taxes to the

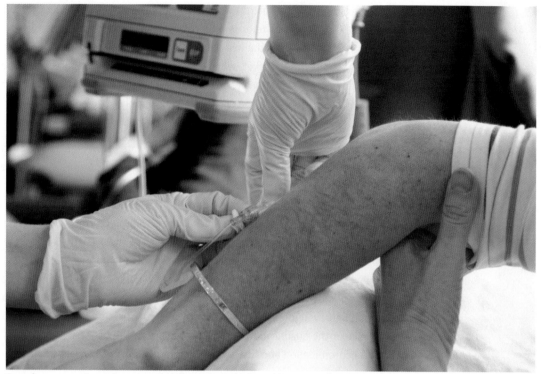

Spending on merit goods such as health results in high positive externalities.

funds necessary to provide them. Because of non-excludability and non-diminishability, no private supplier would offer a public good because it would be unable to exclude free riders. LDCs, with their narrow tax base, find the provision of public goods expensive but very necessary.

Governments also find it necessary to intervene to provide what are called 'mixed' goods and services, which could in principle be treated as private goods, but which do not respond very well to price signals due to a preponderance of externalities. Certain of these goods and services would be under-consumed at market price, because they can be expensive and are not wanted at all times. They are known as **merit goods**, and are high in positive externalities: that is they benefit both the user and non-user. Education and hospital treatment are examples. Spending on education and health produces a literate, numerate and physically fit work-force with consequent benefits in labour productivity, and thus benefit both the direct user and the non-user. Conversely, some goods are **demerit goods**, and their use harms the non-user. The effects of passive smoking on non-users of tobacco provides a well-known example. Other examples include industrial pollution, and the social and economic effects of crime.

Centralisation

Natural monopolies exist where services are more efficiently provided by one supplier than by many. In the case of piped water, sewerage services, and the national grid for electricity distribution, where a huge expensive infrastructure is necessary, the existence of competing suppliers would be a waste of resources involving unnecessary duplication. Economies of scale enjoyed by the single supplier far outweigh any efficiency gains from competition. To prevent the abuse of monopoly power, and to ensure that any producer surplus is returned to the community, it is only 'natural' that the enterprise should be run from the centre, and therefore owned by the state.

The concepts of centralisation and decentralisation are useful when considering the 'proper' degree of government intervention. The distribution and sale of foodstuffs, for example, is best done in a decentralised way; shopkeepers are far better than government officials at detecting the wants and tastes of consumers. In a country like the UK, where the efficiency of retailing has been developed to a fine

degree, no economist in their right minds would advocate the nationalisation of the retail chains such as Sainsbury or Tesco! In the case of telecommunications, where satellite and radio links mean that new technology liberates suppliers from the heavy infrastructure of copper wires, a once natural monopoly is evolving into a very competitive market, where decentralised suppliers are able to respond to consumer wants very quickly indeed. Privatisation in such a situation creates welfare gains, and to modern consumers the situation of 30 years ago where the state had a monopoly of telephone services would seem very strange.

In addition, the privatisation of natural monopolies such as water, sewerage and electricity has been done in the UK, and debate continues over whether this was a wise move. Before this debate is finally settled, the MDCs are busily exporting the idea to the LDCs, and to the new market economies of Eastern Europe, as if the welfare gains of privatisation were a proven fact. If economic development is to improve the human condition in the widest possible sense, then there is surely a central role for government in providing the basic utilities. In the case of merit goods, not even the most enthusiastic free-marketeer would advocate that LDCs should privatise elementary education, as the positive externalities of improved basic literacy are so obviously high. Where there is room for some debate about the role of market prices is with merit goods such as higher education. In this sector of education the private benefits of qualifications at this level, through improved job prospects, perhaps warrant some degree of contribution from the user. Even here, however, if the qualifications are to be relevant to the national programmes for development, then some central co-ordination and hence government planning will always be necessary.

The railways are a classic case of an industry which needs central coordination, and many economists have argued all along that privatisation was an inappropriate policy. In 2009 one railway franchise was taken back into state ownership due to the inability of the franchisee to provide its contracted service. News items have suggested that our motorways are destined to become so overcrowded that emergency services are planning for measures that would have to be implemented in the event of 'gridlock' – traffic jams lasting so long that people would begin to abandon their cars. Is road pricing the answer? Only if governments have the political will to face up to massively unpopular policies, and only if they have the courage to ensure that tax revenue is sufficient to guarantee that public finances are adequate to subsidise viable public transport alternatives to the private motor car. Has privatisation gone so far that governments have surrendered their capability of coordinating transport in an adequate way? In the UK, at least, the evidence of our own eyes would suggest that this is so.

Environmentalists have begun to turn their attention to the low cost airlines, accusing them of causing particular damage to the environment by increasing the frequency of flying and adding to greenhouse gases. While it would appear to be illogical that short haul air journeys in the UK appear often to be so much more attractive to consumers than train travel. But in their defence it can be argued that it is not the fault of the low cost airlines if a relatively high polluting trip by air from Bristol to Edinburgh costs around £40, while a far less polluting trip between the same cities by rail costs several times as much. Rather, it is the fault of successive governments, for the irrational way in which rail privatisation was introduced and has been operated since.

Chapter 16

Why is everyone talking about China?

The China syndrome

When commentators started using the word 'globalisation' on a daily basis, it was often assumed that the word was synonymous with 'Americanisation'. When the average student is asked for an example of globalisation, they will usually name an American company, such as McDonald's or Microsoft. More recently, other commentators, such as Will Hutton of *The Observer* newspaper, and Evan Davis, who has been economics editor of the BBC, have focused on the growing influence of China.

What did you have for Christmas? If it was a mountain bike which cost as little as, say, £70 then there is a strong chance that it was made in China. The Raleigh factory in Nottingham is no longer the centre of the world bicycle industry. If your younger brother or sister had a 'Hogwarts' train set carrying the famous Hornby brand-name, then it was probably not made in Margate, as it once certainly would have been, but in China. On the one hand, something has been lost from UK industrial traditions by such developments. On the other hand British businesses which once seemed totally doomed have survived in some slimmed down shape or form.

Why is it that UK manufacturers find it economic to close their British factories and base their manufacturing in China? The answer is simply that Chinese factory owners can pay as little as £50 a month to workers who come to the manufacturing centres from distant villages, live in dormitory accommodation, and tolerate almost military-style discipline on the factory floor. A product such as a cigarette lighter, for example, which might sell for £12 in the UK can be made for around 50p in China, and still make a millionaire of the Chinese entrepreneur who has the contract to supply outlets in Europe. And China still has workers to spare: in fact, if *all* European and American manufacturing were to re-locate to China, there would still be Chinese workers to spare.

There have been reports of manufacturing companies moving their factories from places like Malaysia to China, thus impoverishing workers in one third world country by moving to a place where labour is even cheaper. And as Chinese incomes and living standards rise, we can confidently predict that factories will re-locate to ever more remote parts of the country, until they eventually abandon China altogether for the new low-wage country of the day.

As Chinese living standards grow, we can expect positive returns in the UK: our steel exports, for example, were for a time revitalised by the demand from Chinese manufacturers, and this will last until China can develop its own steel making capacity. If European motor manufacturers can sell cars to just a small fraction of the Chinese population, then they will have a market of equal size to the saturated markets of Europe. Cheap clothes and similar items from China have been a major contributor to low inflation rates in the UK.

'Globalisation' is not only about goods, but also about services. For example, as Chinese incomes and aspirations rise, the higher education sector in the UK is busy recruiting to first degrees and postgraduate courses such as MBAs among lucrative fee-paying students from China where home universities do not yet have the capacity to satisfy demand. The British Council and Universities UK have estimated that the British economy earns more than £11bn. annually from 'exports' of tuition for foreign students, training, examinations, publishing and educational programming. This places education and training in the same league as exports of oil and financial services. At the present time, there is a shortage of university places within China, and many Chinese students are very keen to spend some time in Europe. British universities have organised 'outreach' programmes located in China, many of which lead to young people from China spending some time studying in the UK.

British businesses found a very different business culture in China.

Britain and China

One problem faced by British businesses when dealing with China is the very different business culture that exists there. For example, Chinese manufacturers often have difficulty in recognising the importance of 'intellectual property' and routinely ignore international treaties on such matters as copyright and patent law. Worse than this casual approach to intellectual property, the Chinese government has in the past been slow to stamp out deliberate counterfeiting, which is a much more sinister and dangerous activity. The passing off as the genuine article of substandard 'pirate' vital components, such as brand name brake linings for motor cars not only undermines the profits of legitimate companies but puts lives at risk.

At the moment Britain is the biggest single source of investment into mainland China. Industrial development and economic growth can cause massive pollution problems, and some of China's waterways are among the most polluted in the world. One of the privatised UK water utility companies gained the contract to build a massive purification plant near Shanghai, and the project appeared to offer guaranteed profits. However like many arrangements with Chinese authorities and enterprises the contract turned out in practice to be worthless, as the institutions which would be expected to regulate business transactions prove to be inadequate, non-existent, or corrupt.

China and the world

At the United Nations Conference on Climate Change in Copenhagen in December 2009, developing countries were offered some funding by the richer countries to help finance a move towards methods of production that produce less greenhouse gas pollution. Although China is officially still classed as a developing country, and although its pollution problems are massive (it is the world's major burner of coal, for example), the Chinese delegation refused this funding. China does not regard itself as a country in need of aid, rather it perceives itself as the leader of what is known as the 'G72' group of less developed countries (Britain belongs to the 'G20' group of countries with high GDPs).

China wishes to develop international relations and is cultivating a particularly strong influence in Africa, where there are reserves of oil, uranium and the base metals that China needs for its continued industrial development. In return for access to these materials, China offers African countries development funding, and African nations appear to prefer this funding to come from China rather than agencies such as the IMF which they see as being dominated by the USA. They believe that Chinese funding comes with fewer strings attached, as China does not insist on, for example, privatisation programmes in return for aid in the same way as the IMF.

Some American politicians have begun to murmur against China in the corridors of power in Washington, and are beginning to question some of the effects of the free trade arrangements that have enabled a country operating a peculiar mixture of neo-communist centralisation and neo-conservative free market liberalisation. There is a growing global phenomenon of '**sovereign wealth fund**', which enables governments to invest in private sector companies around the world. Now that western nations have privatised many of their public utilities, it is ironic that the private sector of the democratic world has become part-owned by the state sector of countries which, in some cases, are among the least democratic and most repressive nations in the world. A proportion of the proceeds of China's export boom has been used in this way.

It can be confidently predicted that such tensions will at some time in the future cause further reactions in the rest of the world, and that China will be increasingly questioned about its economic activities, its contribution to global warming, and such matters as its undemocratic political processes and human rights record.

In December 2009, some of the national leaders' observers who regarded the Copenhagen conference as a failure let it be known that they put the blame on China – for refusing to sign up to legally-binding agreements to reduce emissions. Other observers regarded it as rather ironic that countries that had largely given up on their manufacturing sectors, and were now relying on cheap imports from China, should then criticise China for causing global warming while driving down the costs of those imports.

In due course, we might see calls for restrictions on trade with China, or demands for changes in Chinese behaviour as a condition for China's participation in international institutions. One major global player, Google, has already faced massive international criticism for allegedly agreeing to Chinese government demands for censorship as the price of gaining access to the Chinese market.

Chapter 17

The credit crunch and world recession: what happened?

Economic models

One of the few academic economists who predicted the credit crunch was Professor David ('Danny') Blanchflower, who was a member of the Bank of England's Monetary Policy Committee. At a public lecture at Cardiff University in 2009, Blanchflower was asked by another well-known economist to reveal the secret of his successful prediction: 'What economic policy are you using, Danny? Do please tell us'. The reply was that it was less important to use computer models, but to take part in the 'economics of walking about'.

There is an important message here. Many academic economists have arguably become so theoretical and abstract in their studies that they cannot talk sensibly to the policy makers or to the general public. They can only talk to each other, and when they do so they discuss aspects of what appears to be a branch of mathematics, divorced from the hustle and bustle of everyday life. Everyday life, in fact, is a closed book to them.

Those economists who foresaw the credit crunch were the ones who noticed the illogicality and unsustainability of people using inflationary house prices as a springboard for increasing debt which was used to buy goods which were manufactured by low wage employees in other countries. In the next chapter it is argued that following the credit crunch, as world leaders get to grips with climate change, and realisation sets in that the era of exponential economic growth is over, there will be less concern for quantity and more concern for the quality of life. Less attention will be paid to the acquisition of more and more goods, and more attention paid to the justice and fairness of the distribution of income and wealth. We have already seen the media moving against the high level bankers who received enormous bonuses even as their leadership of the banks had obviously failed. Politicians are beginning to reassess the role of progressive and regressive taxation systems in re-distributing income and wealth. Economists will need to re-assess the nature of their subject of study, and perhaps re-discover the idea of 'political economy'. Those economists who spend their lives with computer models of statistical trends are badly equipped to comment on issues of justice and fairness.

The policy background

As was mentioned in Chapters 4 and 5, the position in macroeconomic policy towards the end of the Twentieth Century was that governments moved away from hands-on macroeconomic management and the Keynesian objective of full employment. They focused instead on managing what was left of the public sector following the privatisation and de-regulation that they inherited from the Thatcher-Reagan years, This meant a move towards liberalisation, reliance on market forces, the idea that markets are rational, that markets clear, and that markets provide maximum utility for consumers. This was reinforced by the collapse of communism and the opening of China and India to international trade.

The global economy is divided into countries that produce, and aim at balance of payments surpluses, (e.g. China, Japan, Germany), and those that consume, and manage apparently permanent balance of payments deficits (e.g. UK, USA, South Africa, Spain, Ireland). How sustainable was this development? Its defenders argued that cheap goods from China would help keep inflation low in the importing countries. Also, China would be recycling its profits into western assets and this supply of currency would push down interest rates, increase borrowing and lead to even more spending. The economist Larry Elliott, a regular columnist for *The Guardian*, has likened this to a perpetual motion machine.

While Gordon Brown was claiming an end to 'boom and bust' the UK economy was relying on three things to keep the economy afloat: financial services, the housing market and the public sector (the latter financed by tax receipts from the other two). But the weak manufacturing sector, together with growing inequality of incomes (the poor borrowing proportionately more than the rich to maintain living standards) exposed the UK to severe problems in the autumn of 2008.

The banking background

It is unfortunate that 'banking' as a focused topic has largely been removed from university and school economics syllabuses because it was no longer regarded as interesting. However, it takes very little effort to understand the awesome extent to which banks create a pyramid of credit, which relies entirely on trust in order to exist. Syllabuses do contain the topic of the investment multiplier, and students who understand this principle can easily gain an understanding of the 'bank credit multiplier'.

Banks exist for three reasons: to accept deposits for safe keeping, to transfer deposits between customers, and to lend money to individuals and businesses. It is their money-lending activities which generate their profits. When they lend, their liquidity (ability to provide cash and other liquid assets) is tied up for the period of the loan, and there is therefore a 'trade off' between liquidity and profitability. Banks find that when they receive a deposit of cash from a customer, that deposit tends to stay in their vaults for a length of time. This is because customers tend to want actual cash only for relatively small transactions, and for larger transactions they will use other means, such as plastic cards, electronic transfers and, to a lesser extent these days, cheques.

Suppose banks find that, on average, a customer who deposits £10 will only come back to withdraw £1 in cash over the counter or from the 'hole in the wall' ATM, and will transfer the other £9 using electronic methods. This means that banks can lend this £9 charging a rate of interest for doing so, and thus earning a profit. Provided the borrower is credit-worthy, then this £9 will be returned in due course, so the contract through which the borrower promises to repay is an asset, but it is not a liquid asset. In this way, if banks are operating with a bank credit multiplier of 10, then every £1 deposited in a bank can be used to support liabilities totalling £10, of which £1 supported by actual cash (a liquid asset), and £9 is supported by promises to repay (illiquid assets). There is a risk here. If customers begin to doubt the soundness of a bank's finances, and all rush to withdraw their cash at once (this is called a 'run' on the bank) then the bank can find that it is short of liquidity, and need to borrow from other banks. In 2007, banks began to distrust each other, and stopped lending to each other. This was because they found that some of their financial products ('derivatives') contained promises to repay from customers who were finding it difficult to repay their loans due to rising interest rates. These were principally 'sub prime' borrowers in the USA who had been encouraged to take out mortgages to buy their houses, even though they were earning too little to truly be able to afford the loan.

The crash

Economists know that 'confidence' is essential for economic growth. The collapse in confidence in the banking sector quickly spread from 'Wall Street to the High Street' and from the financial economy to the real economy. People stopped spending, firms stopped producing, workers were laid off, and the downward spiral of lower production, lower employment, and lower spending, which Keynes had analysed so well in the 1930s began to lead to recession. Suddenly, Keynesian economics was back in fashion.

The technical definition of recession is two successive quarters of negative growth. However, since 6 months is a short time period, and it is possible that a statistical 'blip' might be confused with a genuine economic downturn, some economists have argued that a better definition would cover a time period of a full year. On that basis, recessions are very rare in the UK, happening only eight times since World War II: in 1956 (quarters 2 and 3); 1957 (quarters 2 and 3); 1961 (quarters 3 and 4); 1973 (quarters 3 and 4 and

1974 (quarter 1); 1975 (quarters 2 and 3; 1980 (all four quarters) and 1981 (quarter 1) ; 1990 (quarters 3 and 4) and 1991 (quarters 1, 2 and 3) and 2008 (quarters 2, 3 and 4) and 2009 (quarters 1, 2 and 3). Of these the 2008 and 2009 recessions are easily the worst, measuring between -4.5 and -5.0%, at least 3 percentage points worse than the previous post-war record. At the same time, the massive amounts of money involved in government action were unprecedented. It is estimated that governments spent $30 trillion bailing out the banks, and the UK government's budget deficit grew to the extent that every man, woman and child Britain in effect had a nominal extra debt burden of £5000.

Previous crashes

To those who claim that the current crisis was both unexpected, and unprecedented, Vince Cable, the Liberal Democratic Party's shadow chancellor (and a trained economist) has pointed out that 200 years ago John Stuart Mill described exactly how banking systems collapse. Banks borrow in the short run, lend for the long term, lend too much to customers who cannot repay, and a sudden collapse of confidence leads to recession and unemployment. In the summer of 2007, the world economy began to shudder to a halt when it became clear that American banks and mortgage companies had been lending to people who could barely afford to buy their houses (the 'sub prime' market). This worked when house prices were rising and interest rates were relatively low. However, it could not continue. As interest rates rose more and more borrowers were defaulting on the loans. Meanwhile, the lenders had attempted to insure themselves against their risks, by parcelling up their loans into 'derivative' financial products. When the American bank Lehman Brothers crashed in the autumn of 2008 panic spread around the financial sector as it became clear that many banks had no idea how much of their assets were tied up in these dodgy derivatives. The banking system had become over complicated and over leveraged (too dependent on debt).

Author Gillian Tett has likened financial services as a 'sausage factory linked to a casino'. She argues that sausages are one of the most popular foods in Britain, and making sausages is therefore a good business, but when diseases such as BSE break out the business is undermined if people do not know where the meat comes from. Similarly, banking becomes dangerous if toxic assets are hidden in complicated financial products such as 'credit default swaps' and spread through the banking system so that nobody knows where the time bomb will explode next.

As interest rates rose more borrowers defaulted on their loans.

In the UK it was the Royal Bank of Scotland (RBS) which led the way with this kind of activity, and at the time of its collapse in 2008, in terms of assets on paper it was the largest bank in the world. When the UK government intervened in order to bail out RBS, Northern Rock and other UK institutions, it was said that the whole of the British banking system was in danger of melting down: within 24 hours cashpoints would close and there would be panic in the streets.

Larry Elliott has described how large financial crises follow the same sort of sequence as people often experience when high points in their lives are followed by unexpected crises: a period of exuberance is followed by denial, then grudging acceptance, and finally recovery.

Stephanie Flanders, chief economics correspondent of the BBC, has suggested that by the autumn of 2009 the UK was probably in the early stages of recovery, but it was unclear exactly what shape the recovery would take. There were several possibilities:

- V shaped: a short, sharp recession, followed by a rapid recovery;
- U shaped: a longer recession, bouncing along at the bottom of the graph before recovery;
- W shaped: an early recovery gives a false sense of optimism, another downturn is experienced before a recovery is really achieved;
- L shaped: the economy bounces along the bottom of the activity graph and takes a very long time before there is any sign of an upturn;
- Italicised *L* shaped: things get worse before they slowly improve.

Time will tell later in 2010 which of these has emerged. Vince Cable has pointed out that this recession was different from the Great Crash of 1929 for two reasons:

- In the 1930s, governments did not do anything. This time, governments were willing to nationalise the banks to contain the crisis.

- This time, through the G20 and other international arrangements, governments worked together. In the 1930s, trade barriers and other forms of economic warfare eventually led to military warfare. This time, governments cooperated.

The main strategies that governments used in the short run were:

1. Intervention in the banking sector: nationalising failing banks, encouraging mergers which would normally have been blocked by competition legislation, e.g. the Lloyds Bank acquisition of HBOS.

2. Loose monetary policy: base interest rates falling to near zero; quantitative easing (selling government stock to put liquidity into the economy): in effect, printing more money and putting it into circulation.

3. Fiscal boost: government spending, lower taxes more government borrowing, a larger national debt.

In the longer term, the crisis has left several major issues for the future. Here are four of them:

- The need for an exit strategy. At what point does the government tighten the budget once more? Too soon, and recession returns; too late and world markets lose confidence in the ability of the UK and other countries to service their national debt.

- Banks that are too big to fail are simply too big. Banks need to be reformed, without de-stabilising the banking system.

- A pathway towards growth that is environmentally sustainable and less dependent on financial services. Britain has a poor investment record in terms of both hard infrastructure (railways, roads, etc) and soft infrastructure (education, training, human capital). We are left with insufficient science, engineering and manufacturing.

- Britain cannot achieve recovery alone. We live in a globalised economy. International agreement is required on such issues as requiring banks to keep prudent liquidity/capital ratios, controlling the 'casino' aspects of banks and separating these from personal and business lending,

Conclusion

Confidence in free markets has been shaken. The free market enthusiasts benefitting from the irresponsibility of the banks, and who have been very quick to condemn the public sector and argue for lower taxes, were very quick to appeal to the public sector and accept taxpayers' money to bail them out. It seems that globalisation requires profits to be privatised and losses to be nationalised, which is a distorted view of how free markets operate! Market forces do not guarantee permanent profits. Entrepreneurs need to risk their own money, not that of their unsuspecting customers or of the taxpayer. Failed bankers cannot expect a continuation of their bonus culture. Taxpayers are also voters, and in future elections, when economic and environmental pressures are working against constant economic growth, the electorate are likely to demand that more attention is paid to justice and fairness in the distribution of income.

Chapter 18

Where are we going?

Europe or the open sea?

As the world spins on its axis, at all times of day or night there are financial markets open somewhere in Asia, Europe or North America. New technology means that someone, is always on hand to take your order or accept your payment. Does this mean that the world has become a single market? It is more than half a century since Maynard Keynes proposed the creation of 'Bancor' which, in effect, would have been a world currency. Is the world really any closer to a global currency today? What about free movement of labour? What if I decided to move to, say, Singapore, Texas, or Bali. Would I be welcome? What if I insisted being housed, sending my children to the local school, claiming my pension from the government of the new country, obtaining free healthcare from the local health service, and having my qualifications recognised so that I could walk into a job as similar as possible to the one I have left behind in the UK?

The response to such requests would fall far short of the idealised world of 'globalisation' being claimed by many business leaders and politicians. Some economists (Paul Hirst for example) claim that globalisation is not a useful economic concept and point out that 80 per cent of world trade is carried out between the wealthiest countries of the world and it excludes and disempowers poorer countries. They argue (as we noted earlier) that 'globalisation' is better understood as 'globalism', an attempt to impose a world view rooted in management theory that like its arch-enemy, Marxism, tries to reduce all human relationships to the economic. Furthermore, it can be argued that the internationalisation of financial markets was greater between 1900 and 1914 than it is now. Indeed one can state that international mobility of labour is more difficult to achieve now than it was in the nineteenth century. Also one can assert that the so-called 'Multinational Enterprises' whose activities are often confused with 'globalisation' are actually firmly based in particular countries.

It can be argued that today globalisation is in fact less significant than supranational regionalism – the formation of trading blocs, of which the EU is the most sophisticated example. In Europe we have a single market with free movement of goods and services, free movement of capital, and free movement of labour. The majority of countries belonging to this single market have also signed up to a single currency, to which they either already belong or are committed to join. Many British enthusiasts for 'globalisation' could profitably stop to consider whether their opinions towards this so-called phenomenon are logically consistent with their attitudes towards European integration in general and European Monetary Union in particular.

Where should Britain look for its future trading relations, to the European or the global? Or is this a false choice? Could it be that the EU, with its concerns for more than the purely economic – an international organisation that involves itself with transport, social welfare, the environment, cultural relations, and income distribution (to name but a few of its concerns) – is in fact, despite all its faults, a role model to which the 'globalisers' can only aspire?

Some certainties and possibilities

'Trade' used to signify 'things'. The UK made its fortune during the industrial revolution by trading in heavy objects. Coal was mined and used to make iron and steel which was exported in British-built coal-powered steamships to colonies where British companies used iron and steel to build railways which then needed coal. So we then exported coal. All transactions were made in pounds sterling; a twenty pound note was a wondrous object, almost as large as a writing pad, and the very word 'pound' signified 'weight' while 'sterling' signified something strong, solid and permanent.

The provision of hotel services by poorly paid workers is not the sort of service area where Britain's future lies.

The future lies not so much in 'things' but in 'ideas'. One nineteenth century slogan which still has relevance today is: 'knowledge is power'. In future low wage countries will be the ones where factories stamp out blank CDs and units of digital hardware by the million, using unskilled labour in mass production facilities which can be located anywhere, and where people are easily replaced by machines. When the population of such a country becomes better skilled and educated the search will be on for more sophisticated employment away from the factory floor. High wage countries will be those which have the talent, knowledge and skills to provide the information that is actually stamped on the discs, whether that information takes the form of film, music, computer software or product design.

The distinction between 'goods' and 'services' will become more and more blurred. It is *not* true to say that Britain's future in a globalised world lies in 'services' if the type of service we are thinking about involves the low skills of the part-time de-unionised low wage hotel skivvy or hamburger flipper. Incomes, whether they are generated by goods or services, will be created by trade in 'value added'. Payment for this value added will be electronic and instant. Notes and coins will hardly change hands at all, but will be stored as magnetic blips on bits of plastic (the banking industry in the UK has already announced that it wants to abolish the cheque). In a world where billions of units of value can be transmitted instantly across the globe at any time of day or night by touching a computer screen, currency denominations such as the peso or the pound will simply become ever more irrelevant, and where they persist they will become at best an irritant, at worst an increasingly unacceptable barrier to trade, production and employment. Anyone who doubts this need only take a short trip to any of the poorer countries of Latin America (or even most of the richer ones), where the taxi driver or hotel porter will be delighted to accept a tip in US dollars, but look disconsolately at any offering in their own domestic currency!

Today, 300 million Europeans are receiving their pay, buying their groceries, borrowing money, and saving towards their pensions using a single currency: the euro. Having decided to adhere to the convergence criteria, without yet joining the euro, Britain is in a position to experience all the pain without any of the gain. At the time of writing, late in 2009, however, there is no indication that the political leadership of Britain has any appetite to attempt to lead the British electorate into the Eurozone.

Some predictions

Globalisation, if it means anything, tells us that nation states have to adapt. In many spheres of influence they are too small to compete with multinational enterprises. They must therefore share sovereignty in order to have influence in the world. In some spheres, on the other hand, nation states are too large, and too remote from the localities they attempt to serve, and where their citizens actually live. Throughout Europe, we therefore see in parallel with the upward shift of power, an equally strong downward shift, devolving power towards sub-national regions such as Wales or Scotland. It is possible that people throughout the EU will gradually begin to look to regional government for the microeconomic side of life: transport infrastructure, education services, economic development and so on. They will look to national government for such things as social security, law and order, and fiscal policy. And it is logical to conclude that the general macroeconomic framework, including interest rates, anti-inflation policy and world trading relations, will increasingly be set at the supranational level of the regional bloc, with an EU of at least 27 and perhaps over 30 members. Of these members, the Premier League will consist of those countries which belong to the euro, with a Division 1 ready to join and waiting to qualify, and a Division 2 ruled out (or ruling themselves out) of the major championships for the foreseeable future.

To which division will the UK belong? That is largely in the hands of the British people themselves.

One thing is absolutely certain. Having just about survived the effects of the credit crunch, before very long the global economy will need to face the coming oil crunch. A time is fast approaching when the UK and other industrial countries around the globe will need to seek alternatives to their heavily oil-dependent economies. In Britain's case, alternatives are needed in more than one sense, since the UK recently shifted from being a net oil exporter to a net oil importer for the first time in over a decade.

Meanwhile, Britain's balance of trade deficit is as large as it has ever been in 300 years, and thousands of manufacturing jobs continue to disappear each year. Such trends hardly indicate that Britain is taking full advantage of 'globalisation'. In order to do this, the lessons of the credit crunch need to be learned, and the UK economy needs to be rebalanced, away from consumption, importing, financial services, house price inflation, borrowing, privatisation and dependency on resource use for constant growth. Instead the balance needs to be shifted towards investment, exporting, manufacturing, affordable housing, saving, sound public infrastructure, environmental conservation and justice and fairness in the distribution of income.

Recommended further reading

Amin, Ash; Thrift, Nigel: *Globalisation, Institutions and Regional Development in Europe*, Oxford.

Atwood, Margaret: *Payback: Debt and the Shadow Side of Wealth*, Bloomsbury.

Beck, Ulrich: *What is Globalisation?*, Polity Press.

Black, Ian: *The UK Economy 1999-2009*, Anforme.

Branson, Richard; Greenspan, Alan; Sen, Armatya; et.al.: *Globalisation Laid Bare: Lessons in International Business*, Gibson Square Books.

Cable, Vince: *The Storm*, Atlantic Books.

Chomsky, Noam, *Profit Over People*, Seven Stories Press.

Clift, Peter; Drury, Spencer; Simpson, Gavin: *Ten Top Topics in International Trade and Globalisation*, Anforme.

Cramp, Peter; Keefe, James: *Revision Guide for A2 Level Economics*, Anforme.

Dicken, Peter: *Global Shift: The Internationalisation of Economic Activity*, Chapman.

Dunkley, Graham: *The Free Trade Adventure*, Zed Books.

Earth Island Press, *The Case Against Free Trade*, North Atlantic Books.

Elliott, Larry; Atkinson, Dan: *The Gods That Failed*, The Bodley Head.

Ethicalconsumer.org, *The Good Shopping Guide*, Sankey.

Friedman, Thomas: *The Lexus and the Olive Tree*, First Anchor.

Friedman, Thomas: *Hot, Flat and Crowded: Why We Need a Green Revolution*, Farrar, Straus and Giroux.

Gavin, Brigid: *The European Union and Globalisation*, Edward Elgar.

Giddens, Anthony: *Runaway World*, Profile.

Gray, John: *After Social Democracy*, Demos.

Gray, John: *False Dawn: The Delusions of Global Capitalism*, Granta Books.

Haas, Peter, (ed.): *Environment in the New Global Economy*, Edward Elgar.

Harford, Tim: *The Undercover Economist*, Oxford University Press.

Harvey, Mark; Quilley, Steve; Beynon, Huw: *Exploring the Tomato: Transformations of Nature, Society and Economy*, Edward Elgar.

Hertz, Noreena: *The Silent Takeover: Global Capitalism and the Death of Democracy*, Arrow Books.

Hertz, Noreena: *IOU: The Debt Threat and Why We Must Defuse It*, Fourth Estate.

Hirst, Paul; Thompson, Grahame: *Globalisation in Question*, Polity Press.

Hobsbawm, Eric: *Globalisation, Democracy and Terrorism*, Abacus.

Hutton, Will: *The World We're In*, Little, Brown.

Hutton, Will: *The Writing on the Wall: China in the Twenty-first Century*, Little, Brown.

Jacques, Martin: *When China Rules the World*, Penguin.

Klein, Naomi: *No Logo*, Flamingo.

Lawson, Neal, *All Consuming*, Penguin.

Legrain, Philippe: *Open World: The Truth About Globalisation*, Abacus.

Legrain, Philippe: *Immigrants: Your Country Needs Them*, Abacus.

MacGillivray, Alex: *A Brief History of Globalisation*, Robinson Publishing.

Monbiot, George: *The Age of Consent*, Flamingo.

Patel, Raj: *The Value of Nothing: How to Reshape Market Society and Redefine Democracy*, Portobello Books.

Porter, Michael: *The Competitive Advantage of Nations*, Free Press.

Ransom, David: *The No-Nonsense Guide to Fair Trade*, Verso.

Romer, Stephen: *The Year in Review and Revision Guide 2009-2010*, Anforme.

Smith, Charles; Rees, Gareth: *Economic Development*, Palgrave.

Smith, Charles; Smith, Matthew; Etherington, Ian: *Revision Express: Economics*, Pearson/Longman.

Stiglitz, Joseph: *Globalisation and its Discontents*, Norton.

Stiglitz, Joseph: *Making Globalisation Work*, Norton.

Tett, Gillian: *Fool's Gold: How the Geeks Broke the Banks*, Little, Brown.

Toynbee, Polly; Walker, David: *Unjust Rewards: Ending the Greed That is Bankrupting Britain*, Granta Books.

Turner, Graham: *The Credit Crunch: Housing Bubbles, Globalisation and the Worldwide Economic Crisis*, Pluto Press.

Webster, Ken; Johnson, Craig: *Sense and Sustainability: Educating for a Low Carbon World*, TerraPreta.

Wilkinson, Richard; Pickett, Kate: *The Spirit Level: Why More Equal Societies Almost Always Do Better*, Allen Lane.

Useful blogs, podcasts, websites

David Smith
http://economicsuk.com/blog/

Evan Davis
http://www.bbc.co.uk/blogs/today/evandavis/

New Economics Foundation
http://www.neweconomics.org/

New Internationalist
http://www.newint.magazine.co.uk/globalization/

Nigel Tree
http://www.anforme.co.uk/blog/

Peter Day
http://www.bbc.co.uk/podcasts/series/worldbiz/

Richard Young
http://rapidrevision.co.uk/economics-student/

Robert Peston
http://www.bbc.co.uk/blogs/thereporters/robertpeston/

Stephanie Flanders
http://www.bbc.co.uk/blogs/thereporters/stephanieflanders/

Index